G000280610

WILLIAM KENT
Landscape garden designer

AN ASSESSMENT AND CATALOGUE OF HIS DESIGNS

Bartholomew Dandridge,
William Kent, circa.1730,
National Portrait Gallery

WILLIAM KENT
Landscape garden designer
AN ASSESSMENT AND CATALOGUE OF HIS DESIGNS

John Dixon Hunt

ARCHITECTS IN PERSPECTIVE
Series Editor: Peter Willis

A. Zwemmer Limited

For Michael and Alice Leslie

© 1987 John Dixon Hunt

First published 1987 by A. Zwemmer Ltd
A subsidiary of Philip Wilson Publishers Ltd
26 Litchfield Street
London WC2H 9NJ

Distributed in the USA by
A. Zwemmer Ltd
Harper & Row, Publishers, Inc
10 East 53rd Street
New York NY 10022

ISBN 0 302 00600 1
LC 87–061181

Designed by Gillian Greenwood
Typeset and printed by Jolly & Barber Ltd, Rugby
and bound by Dorstel Press Ltd

Contents

List of illustrations in the text

Preface

This book contains the revised text of the Ferens Fine Art Lectures, which I was invited to deliver at the University of Hull in January 1985. It was an honour to be the Ferens lecturer, and I am most grateful to the University of Hull for its invitation, which allowed me to develop and set out my ideas on the landscape designs of William Kent during the tercentennial year of his birth.

Previous studies of William Kent (by Margaret Jourdain and Michael I. Wilson) sought to survey all aspects of their subject's multifarious activities as architect, furniture and interior designer, painter and book illustrator. The only exhibition devoted to Kent during the tercentenary also chose, as far as it was able, to present him as a many-sided artist. By contrast, my book isolates and highlights Kent's work as a landscape designer: this is in part simply because there alone am I competent enough to make any contribution, but also because this particular aspect of his career raises specific problems which do not arise with his architectural or decorative work.

Any discussion of Kent's contribution to English garden history has to cope with the fact that only one garden by him survives anything like intact – Rousham, near Oxford – and even that, like many others, had been worked upon first by another designer; the main burden of any analysis therefore rests upon the surviving drawings. Accordingly, I have divided this study into three sections: the first sketches the often rather shadowy contexts in which Kent's career as landscape designer must be seen – his knowledge of Italian gardens, his ambitions as a history painter, and his work in the theatre; the second focuses upon the corpus of landscape drawings; the third considers the surviving landscapes by Kent, with particular attention being given to his *chef-d'oeuvre*, Rousham.

The Vice-Chancellor of the University of Hull and Lady Marshall were the kindest and most relaxing of hosts on the occasion of my visits; to Professor John Wilton-Ely and Professor Jay Appleton I was also grateful for hospitality, encouragement and support (including the making of slides). For some last-minute assistance in obtaining materials for my lectures I must also thank both Tom Francis and Peter Bacon. And my gratitude and thanks, finally, to those members of my audience who braved the most intolerable weather to attend my lectures.

I have kept the structure of the original four lectures, though dividing them somewhat differently into chapters. I also have removed traces of oral delivery and taken the opportunity to augment discussions in the final two sections for which there was not sufficient time during the lectures. In addition I have provided a catalogue of Kent's landscape drawings; since none exists, my analysis of his work was necessarily based upon a thorough survey of all his surviving designs which it seemed useful to present in the form of a catalogue in the hope that others will be able to build upon it. References to illustrations in the text refer either to this catalogue where each item is reproduced (cited as cat. no. 1, etc.) or to other plates in the text (1, etc.).

I have incurred many obligations in the course of this book: above all to the various institutions where Kent drawings are preserved and their curators: I would especially like to thank for their help and interest Mr Peter Day, Keeper of Collections at Chatsworth, and Mr F. C. Jolly, Administrator of the Holkham Estate. Friends and colleagues have also aided me in various ways: Kenneth Woodbridge, John Harris, Robert Williams, Andor Gomme, Peter Willis, Michael Symes and, especially, Howard Colvin, whose generous and careful reading of a final draft of the book pruned it of much error.

1 Countess of Burlington (perhaps Kent), pencil portrait of William Kent writing at desk, Trustees of the Chatsworth Settlement

Introduction

William Kent was born towards the end of 1685 and baptised on 1st January 1686 (new style) at St Mary's parish church in Bridlington, Yorkshire.[1] We know virtually nothing about his family or its circumstances. His father, another William, spelt his name 'Cant'. We presume that the father and mother were not well off, but even that is a deduction from the account of Kent given by George Vertue: 'His parents' or friends' circumstances not being in a condition to forward his practice and the expenses of a profession...'[2] Otherwise we know so little of Kent's early years that his recent biographer, Michael I. Wilson, scatters 'probably's and 'no doubt's rather profusely as he begins his narrative; it seems pointless to add any more suppositions. We can, however, securely deduce from Kent's mature writing and remarks that his early education in Yorkshire was minimal, whatever he may have acquired in later life: hence perhaps his friend Alexander Pope's mischievous description of him as 'a wild Goth... from a country which has never been held no part of Christendom'.[3]

Biographers often unconsciously adopt models for their narratives (Pope's remark itself conceals a cultural model to which further reference will be made). The notes that George Vertue left about Kent may be no exception: the provincial lad made good in the metropolis (the Dick Whittington syndrome), as well as the more general notion of the child as father of the man, structure Vertue's account of Kent's early career. We are told that the young William was one of 'those, who in Arts, in their early dawns of Life shew a Natural Genius in drawing, Especially, which is the root and foundation of fruitful Genius'; further, having 'when young... unexpectedly... demonstrated his youthful inclinations to drawing', he was rescued from an apprenticeship to a 'coach painter. & house painter' by some prosperous Yorkshiremen. They raised money for Kent's studies, 'recommended him to proper persons at London', and from there he was sent to Italy.[4]

He travelled with John, son of the architect William, Talman, and with Daniel Lock, an amateur artist and also perhaps an architect. It was Kent's ambition to become a painter, and he almost certainly trained himself by entering the studio of an established painter in Rome, the centre for all aspiring artists at this time: in 1714 he announced to one of his patrons, Burrell Massingberd, whom he must have met two years earlier while Massingberd was on the Grand Tour, that he was working under Giuseppe Chiari, a pupil of Carlo Maratti.[5] He would have copied old pictures as well as painted some himself, and in 1713 he gained the Pope's medal as the second prize in the annual competition organised by the Accademia di S. Luca.[6] He executed a ceiling fresco for the church of S. Giuliano dei Fiamminghi, which survives, and sent back to Chicheley Hall, Buckinghamshire, another panel for Sir John Chester, a friend of Massingberd.[7]

It would be as a painter that Kent first made his way once he returned to England in 1719. Although he proved to be a very disappointing artist, it is clear that his Italian training as well as his ambition to succeed in this branch of the fine arts exercised a lingering hold upon him and seems to have determined some of his ideas and techniques as a landscape designer. It will be necessary, therefore, to take up his painterly career as one of the contexts for his landscape work, above all to see if it is possible to adjudicate in what fashion his so-called 'picturesque' designs derived from his early dedication to pictures in Italy.

But it is also in Italy that Kent's architectural interests began and were developed, as well as his involvement in designing for the theatre. Kent was by all accounts too energetic and omnivorous to have confined himself to the study of paintings alone. His Thursdays, at least in the first few years in Rome, were set aside for sightseeing with Talman and Lock – 'curiosity' days.[8] And on these occasions he saw and sketched buildings, towns and (we must assume) gardens. He would have got to know Rome in great detail as well as its neighbouring hilltowns like Tivoli and Frascati. He journeyed further afield, too, as companion, guide or agent for patrons, and so managed to visit at one time or another all of the major sites on the Grand Tour – Naples, Genoa, Bologna, Florence, Siena, Lucca, as well as the Veneto and the Italian Lakes. By 1717 he would claim to 'have seen all Italy'.[9] Even if he could not have anticipated how much time he would give to garden designs in England in the 1730s and 1740s, it is inconceivable that Kent would not have taken the opportunity to visit and study some major examples of Italian Renaissance garden art: his English designs make specific allusions, as we shall see, to villa gardens at both Rome and Frascati. In 1715 Massingberd was even asking Kent's advice on a summer house which he planned to build and decorate with Kent's assistance; Kent sketched a plan in his reply, the first of many garden buildings he would invent (cat. no. 59).

But it was two other patrons, Thomas Coke, heir to Holkham in Norfolk, and Richard Boyle, the third earl of Burlington, who must have contributed most to developing his architectural interests. In 1714 he accompanied the former on a tour of northern Italy, and kept a journal of their visits which includes an enthusiastic memorandum on the Medici garden of Pratolino (see 2): that this should be the only garden which Kent specifically praises and records in any detail should give pause to those garden historians who, following Walpole's lead, want to claim him as the father of 'natural gardening'.[10] Kent was travelling north of Rome again in 1714, and three years later began his journey home to England with visits to Florence and Genoa. At the latter he met up with Burlington, whom he had first encountered in Rome in 1714 and who was now en route for Vicenza and Venice. It is improbable that when Burlington took him to view 'two fine palaces of Vitruvio in Genova',[11] these two were not also tempted by the fine garden and grottoes which had always attracted Englishmen upon their first entry into Italy at Genoa.[12]

Otherwise, we catch glimpses of Kent's Italian years through John Talman's letters, a few of Kent's (though unfortunately he seems to have been a bad correspondent) and in his very fragmentary diary of the tour with Coke in 1714.[13] Most of these references focus upon his main role in Italy – copying pictures for his sponsors and their friends back in England, sending home paintings, drawings and engravings, scouting out and purchasing *objets d'art*, of which antique items were the most prized, let alone undertaking such odd jobs as obtaining Naples soap, fans and dictionaries for Massingberd.[14]

The importance of these years in Italy for Kent's subsequent career cannot be under-estimated. Never one, despite his humble origins, to be in awe of people like Coke or Burlington, he confirmed himself in what Coke called the 'language and the virtuosoship'

2 Detail of page from Kent's journal of an Italian journey in 1714, with his entry on Pratolino, Bodleian Library, Oxford

of Italy.[15] Furthermore, it was almost entirely through contacts made in Italy that he acquired the influential patrons who employed him after his return and recommended him to their friends.

Above all, it is clear that the whole inspiration of Italy meant much to Kent: not for nothing was he known as the 'signior' or 'Kentino'. He was a prime example of that persistent phenomenon, the Englishman whose visit to Italy forever afterwards holds him in its thrall: he adopts Italian airs and mannerisms, lards his speech and his correspondence with Italian phrases, refers to himself and is addressed as 'Giuglielmo', models his imaginative as well as social conduct on memories of those golden years when he enjoyed the good fortune of being in that superlative ambience of Italian art, architecture, culture, landscape and history. For our purposes, nothing better underlines the contemporary acknowledgement of the superiority of Italy than the frequent claim that it was 'the Garden of the World'.[16] It was therefore inevitable that when Kent came to design for English estates he would recall (as he did in his architectural work) the example of Italy – actual Italian gardens in that paradisal world where he had spent the best part of ten years. It is these, then, that are arguably the prime context for his landscape work.

London oct: y 24. 1745

My Lord

I reciev'd your letter of y 15 Ins: and
the note upon m. Hoare of one hunderd pounds
of which sum I have paid to m. Mary Harvy
or order this morning — the best news I can
tell you an express is come that Ld Albermarl
& Troops are landed at Sheelds & Jch. Wade is
on his March, so its hoped in a little time whe
shall here the Ribels will be dispers'd or destroy'd
the zeal thats shewd in every county to raise
men, makes me believe my Ld Ailisbury will do
the like & be a Capt —

I met D. mead he enquir'd much how you all doe
he has sent me a book wrote by Mons. Bianchini
to look over, its account of what was found in
year twenty in the Fernese Garden on Mont
Palatine with Plans of y rooms &c. but they have
imagined uprights alla Romanesco — as politicks are
not my Genius, it diverts me much now at nights
to look & read of these fine remaines of Atiquity

I hope you are all
well & think now its
time to come this way

yours Wm Kent

3 Kent letter to Lord Burlington of 24
October 1745, on excavations in Rome,
Trustees of the Chatsworth Settlement

1 Contexts for Kent's work as landscape designer

Italy and Italian gardens

The materials we have to chart Kent's acquaintance with Italian gardens are meagre. But we do have a great deal of information about how other English visitors responded to villas and gardens and we may assume that the patterns and habits of the Grand Tour developed throughout the seventeenth century found further expression in Kent too.[1]

Three themes dominate the English response to Italian gardens in the hundred years before William Kent's own visit. The most important was the relationship of modern Renaissance gardens to their classical predecessors: in the virtual absence of anything that could be confidently identified as surviving antique examples, these were imagined on the basis of a usually somewhat tendentious reading of descriptions in Latin literature. The second theme was the fascinating variety that was noticed in Italian gardens; a variety of styles and forms in different parts of Italy as well as a variety of formal elements within any one specific example; this interest in Italian garden diversity was closely associated with the relationships that were seen to exist between villa gardens and their immediate rural surroundings. The third theme, to be considered in section two in the context of Kent's work for the theatre, was the connection between gardens and theatres and the theatrical ambience of Italian gardens even when they contained no actual theatrical space.

Kent was by no means well educated and one cannot imagine him reading carefully through Latin authors, as Joseph Addison did a few years earlier, to compile an anthology of passages describing their gardens and landscapes which he could then use to compare with the actual 'face of the countryside'.[2] But his patrons were fascinated by the antique world, collected its statues and studied its architectural remains. So given Kent's voracious appetite for things Italian, it seems fairly safe to assume that something of this fascination for the classical past, including gardens, rubbed off on him. Certainly, late in his career, in a letter to Lord Burlington (3), he referred to a work on excavations, including some beneath the Orti Farnesiani on the Palatine Hill, that had been sent to him by Dr Mead who owned several of the antique statues found during those digs. Kent's comment is that since he is bored by politics 'it diverts me much now at nights to look & read of these fine remains of Atiquety (*sic*)'.[3]

Direct knowledge of classical gardens was, of course, meagre, though guides pointed out remains of what they wanted visitors to think were ancient villas. But engraved reconstructions of Roman buildings, as well as maps which marked the supposed sites of villas and gardens (among other items) which were well known from literary sources could be purchased in Rome itself. Thus Basil Kennett's *Romae Antiquae Notitia*, a fifth edition of which was published while Kent was in Italy, discusses the location in modern Rome of such gardens as Sallust's, citing the relevant Latin texts in his notes.[4] Sequences of such books throughout the seventeenth century had alerted English visitors to the sites (whether actual or supposed mattered little) of classical gardens. When Richard Lassels, the author of a much valued guide book to Italy, visited Frascati, the Roman Tusculum, he knew that 'here Cato was born, here Lucullus delighted himself, and Cicero studied'. Or at Mola, where Cicero had another villa, an anonymous traveller of 1675 found 'several Grottoes with fountains in the sollid rock, divers Archt Vaults, with his place of Burial . . . the garden close by the sea, and now full of tall Orange-trees'.[5] No wonder some travellers expressed scepticism at the identification of such sites: the future Bishop Burnet visiting the Naples area in 1685–86 recorded the remains of 'Cicero and Virgil's Houses, for which there is nothing but a dubious tradition'.[6]

4

Such habits of viewing the Italian landscape obviously persisted into Kent's time. His companion in Rome, John Talman, who was there on his second visit, tells in one letter that he has purchased the 'Old Rome of Pirro Ligorio in 10 sheets', and this plan included representations of gardens like that with descending terraces shown on the Pincian Hill (4). Talman had also taken notice of another publication which located antique buildings on a contemporary street plan.[7] Typical of this interest is an item in the collections at Chatsworth that originated with Burlington; it is a volume of drawings entitled *Antiquae Urbis Praeclarissima Aedificia. . .* and seems to be a series of copies in brown wash of engraved reconstructions of classical buildings which were widely available. Some pages in the Chatsworth volume note gardens or *horti* (5) as being associated with these reconstructed buildings; but we know that many remains of Roman architecture were linked in the Renaissance with gardens when in fact no such connection had existed. Even such an authority on antique buildings as Andrea Palladio thought that the Temple of the Sun had stood in a garden in ancient times.[8] The Chatsworth album simply serves to

4 Pirro Ligorio, detail of reconstructed plan of ancient Rome, sixteenth-century engraving

5a and **5b** Drawings of reconstructions of Roman buildings with gardens, from Chatsworth Drawings vol. xxxvii (*Antiquae Urbis Praeclarissima Aedificia*), Trustees of the Chatsworth Settlement

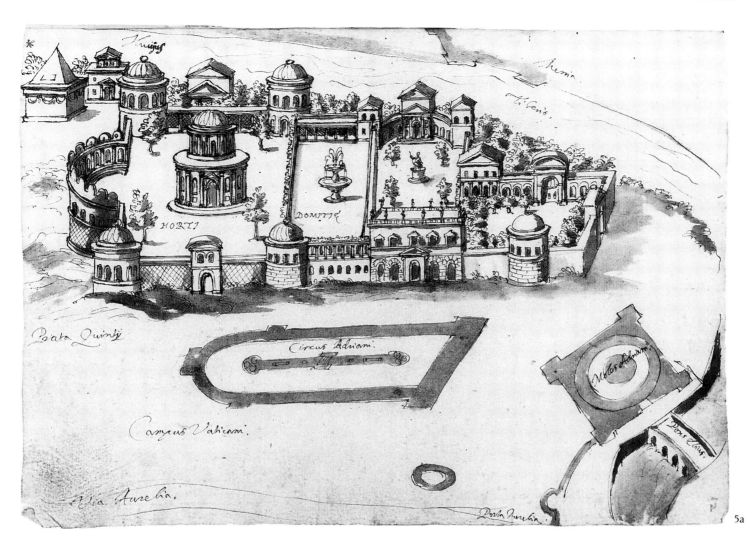

5a

5b

illustrate both the enormous interest there was in reconstructing Roman architecture and how the less than systematic study of classical remains contributed to creative confusions in their interpretation and subsequent re-use.

The palimpsest of urban Rome therefore yielded juxtapositions which are of consequence for Kent's garden designs. Ancient buildings provided with modern gardens whether or not they would originally have had them are surely echoed in several of Kent's designs (see cat. nos 22 and 43). Similarly, the fact that many Roman remains were half buried in the ground contrived some unexpected effects, especially when modern gardens had been created around them. Travellers before Kent had remarked specifically upon the loggia or grotto effect created at the Villa Barberini at Albano (see also 6 and 7): in 1691 William Bromley visited 'pleasant gardens, large Caves in the Rocks . . . and by the Walls, on each side the Garden, are Ruines of ancient Baths, as is guessed from so much as remains'.[9] A somewhat later traveller, Edward Wright, reveals a far more sophisticated response:

> the *Villa Barberini* . . . was once the Villa of *Pompey*. Here were what they called *Horti Pensiles*, Gardens made upon Portico's, which were brought down in several Descents one below another, to the Lake on that side of the Hill. The like were on the other side, towards *Albano*, where the Porticoes do many of them now remain. There is one long and large Portico, which has some Remains of the old Painting now on its Vault, with Ornaments of Stucco.[10]

6 Remains of ancient baths and modern gardens in Rome, engraving from Alexandri Donati, *Roma vetus ac Recens . . .*, 1694

7 Jonathan Skelton, *The villa of Maecenas at Tivoli*, 1750s, Birmingham City Art Gallery

8 The Temple of Ancient Virtue, Stowe
(*photo: R. & H. Chapman*)

Kent recalls similar effects in his landscape work, above all when he constructed the Praeneste Terrace at Rousham, which, as its name indicates, is an allusion to the ruined Temple of Fortune at the modern Palestrina.

Kent's borrowings from classical buildings for his garden designs usually seized upon only a detail of a ruin or an imaginary reconstruction from a source such as the Chatsworth volume, rather than adopted a whole layout; or, alternatively, extrapolated from sources unrelated to gardens. It was not for nothing that Kent's sketches and designs show a fondness for the *capriccio*.[11] The Temple of Ancient Virtue at Stowe (8) is a familiar example of how Kent could invoke for English garden purposes a classical building

unrelated to Roman gardens, the so-called Temple of the Sybil at Tivoli (9). But another circular temple, only partly surviving, also existed at Tivoli and was indeed part of Hadrian's elaborate landscape garden (10). In the eclectic and creative confusions which seem to mark many of Kent's sources for his garden designs it is quite conceivable that he was thinking of both Tivoli temples, one of which – Hadrian's – was associated with as beautiful a valley as the one he was decorating in the Elysian Fields at Stowe. Other echoes and allusions may be detected in his drawings or completed designs: the Temple of Venus at Stowe seems in part just a miniaturised Palladio-like structure; but it alludes more specifically to several antique exedral buildings that survived in the landscape of modern Rome and were related to gardens as well as to published reconstructions of classical gardens (see 5).

9 Gaspar van Wittel, called Vanvitelli, *Landscape with the (so-called) Temple of the Sybil, Tivoli,* Viscount Coke and the Trustees of the Holkham Estate

But there were, of course, other ways in which the Italian gardens that Kent saw were eloquent of their vanished classical predecessors. The most important of these was their decoration with either the sculptural spoils of antique gardens or copies of them. Yet in this respect, too, what Renaissance gardens considered apt decoration did not necessarily derive from gardens in Roman times. The fine items of sculpture around which the Vatican created its Belvedere gardens in the early sixteenth century – the Laöcoon, Romulus and Remus, the river gods Nile and Tiber and the so-called Cleopatra – were not classical garden statues.[12] But this Belvedere sculpture garden, supported by many literary accounts of sculpture in ancient gardens, spawned a series of modern imitations. This tradition of sculpture gardens after what was thought of as the Roman model and decorated with real or imitation classical items persisted up to the time of Kent's stay in

10 Temple above the so-called Vale of Tempe in the grounds of Hadrian's Villa, Tivoli (*photo: Georgina Masson*)

Rome. English travellers responded enthusiastically to antique sculpture because, as one of them put it, 'marbles . . . speak *Roman* history more palpably than any author'.[13]

That William Kent was a serious student of Roman history is unlikely. But the formal (as opposed to the intellectual) excitements of Italian sculpture gardens – their repertoire of artificial shapes set against natural backgrounds – certainly made their impression upon him. One particular subject of classical statuary much imitated in Renaissance gardens was the river god: his presence intimated in allegorical fashion the 'source' of the specific waters over which he presided, alluded to the neighbouring rivers which maybe fed a rich man's gardens, and generally added a distinctly antique touch to a modern garden. Such modern statues were modelled upon celebrated examples discovered during the Renaissance, but acquired extra force by their clear visualisation of such famous passages in Latin literature as that in which Father Tiber greeted Aeneas on his arrival upon Italian shores.[14] One of Kent's sketches for the hillside at Chatsworth involves such a river god in his *capriccio* (cat. no. 6). And Kent's friend, Alexander Pope, planned but never executed a design for his river front at Twickenham where two river gods with accompanying mottoes would have established Pope's place in traditions of poetry and country retreat: the learning of that scheme may be Pope's, but its proposed manipulation of Italianate imagery seems very Kentian.[15]

Kent's drawings of Burlington's gardens at Chiswick may declare his patron's taste as much as his own. But their invocation of classicising sculpture is an evident delight of Kent's own, as his drawings reveal. And this delight was both a pleasure in the shapes and forms which statuary lent to gardens and a distinct echo of many Italian gardens seen between 1709 and 1719. We know Kent worked at the Villa Ludovisia (11) while he was in Rome;[16] its gardens were especially esteemed, not only for their creation on the supposed site of 'the Viridarium of the Poet Sallust' (as Evelyn reported), but for their plein-air museum. Evelyn in 1644 described how the large 'garden is in every quarter beset with antique statues, and Walkes planted with Cypresse, at the extreme of one, stands a Bassrelievo of white marble very antient & good'; while some fourteen years later Francis Mortoft expressed his pleasure with 'A Gallery, as they call it, which is like a Laborinth running out of one round into another and cut soe prettily that one shall hardly see any other garden in such a fashion, and at least 100 Roman statues about these Cutts'.[17] Such an eloquent revival of antiquity in a modern garden clearly had great attraction for gardenists like Kent. If by the time of his visit the sheer profusion of classical debris, what one traveller termed rather wearily a 'ware-house'[18] of sculpture, seemed overwhelming and even meaningless, that too provided inspiration for English garden art. Pope's friend, Joseph Spence, wrote his book *Polymetis* to try and identify the numerous Roman deities. His eponymous character explains how he has created a landscape full of temples, each of which houses statues and accompanying documentation – literary descriptions and medals – which will elucidate the confusions of Roman deities.[19] Spence provides a literal solution to the perplexities that English travellers in Rome expressed when confronted with some of its extensive sculpture collections. So Veryard confessed that 'If antient *Rome* had Thirty thousand Gods as *Varro* assures us it had, I am confident one might find a Limb of each in some part or other of this Palace'.[20] Kent's playful use of classical statuary in some of his drawings has clear affinities with these contemporary attitudes to the profusion and meanings of antique sculpture.

11 Gardens of the Villa Ludovisia, Rome, from Falda, *Li Giardini di Roma*, 1683

At a more serious level of response was the attempt to extrapolate classical garden designs from Latin texts. Again, Joseph Spence, whom Pope and therefore presumably Kent knew well, provides an example. He was attracted by an attempt to reconstitute Horace's Sabine farm from allusions to it in his poetry; all the relevant quotations are provided with a commentary on what could be deduced from them.[21] It is all very tendentious. That Horace 'had that taste for wild natural gardening which has obtained so much among us of late' is by no means proven from stray remarks in his poems. The spring of water near Horace's house ('tecto vicinus aquae fons') is glossed as bursting out of the hillside, a natural fountain; but there is nothing to suggest that it was not in fact shaped architecturally.

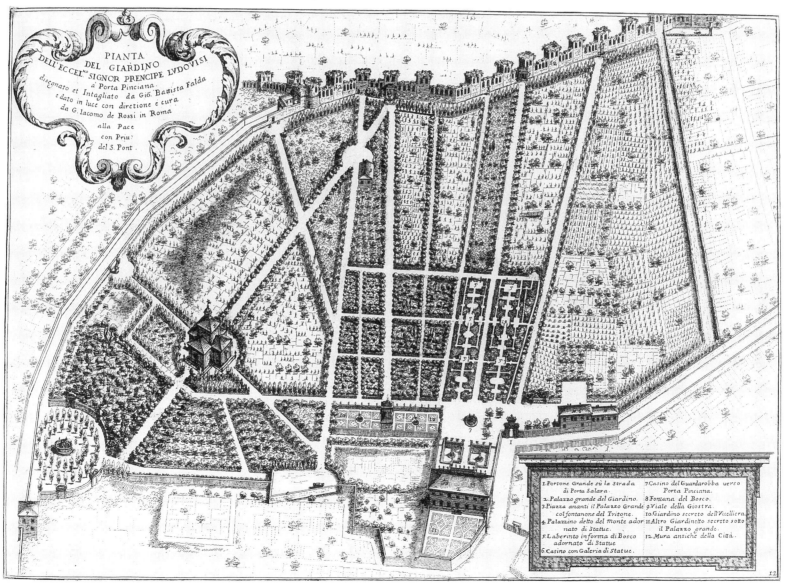

Such contemporary adjudications of classical texts in the light of modern tastes and assumptions also characterised the Burlington circle within which Kent resided. And its clearest manifestation, at least in garden terms, was a publication dedicated to Burlington in 1726, Robert Castell's *The Villas of the Ancients Illustrated*. Castell deliberately sets out what must have been the habitual and unconscious mental process of many English visitors to Italy. He surveys certain key Latin texts on gardens and garden buildings, notably the younger Pliny's letters on his two villas in Tuscany and Laurentium, near Ostia. He provides a commentary upon their significance and interprets their texts in both verbal and visual modes: thus his plans propose actual layouts of villa and garden as deduced from Pliny's literary descriptions. Castell's method is careful and scholarly enough, but it is equally clear that these plans declare as much the landscape ideas of the Burlington group as any archaeological accuracy. In particular we should notice the incorporation of 'natural' or 'rural' territories within the space of the villa complex.[22] Pliny certainly wrote of a part of his Tuscan estate that it suddenly presented a 'rural imitation' in the midst of the more organised garden ('in opere urbanissimo subita velut illati ruris imitatio'). This has clearly been interpreted by Castell in the light of current ideas and taste, among which we should give priority to the experience of modern Italian villa complexes visited on the Grand Tour by Burlington and Kent among others.[23]

Castell's reconstruction of antique villas also gives prominence to the involvement, the interpenetration, of villas and their surrounding agricultural land. Classical texts and modern Italian experience combined to promote an idea of the country house set in its varied landscape, an idea which was to have an enormous effect on the development of the landscape garden under Kent and his successors. Again, it is Joseph Spence who can take us economically into this topic. When he came in the mid eighteenth century to explain the origins of Philip Southcote's so-called *ferme ornée* at Woburn, he traced them to memories of the Italian countryside – 'fields', as he put it, 'going from Rome to Naples'.[24] It is clear that tourists like Spence did not look at fields between Rome and Naples with innocent eyes; as Addison had done in his influential *Remarks on several parts of Italy*, first published in 1705 and revised in 1718, they compared the face of the country with passages in Latin literature. This in its turn led them to read the Italian landscape in terms of Virgil's *Georgics* or the writings of Varro, Columella and Pliny. Addison's own commentary on the *Georgics* stressed Virgil's vision of the fruitfulness of all Italy and uses about it the language of garden art (notably, 'vales and grottos') which linguistically endorses the cliché that Italy was the garden of the world. Many parts of the country caused travellers to exclaim how garden-like it was: the roads of the Veneto were like 'walks in a garden'; around Lucca it was 'one continued Garden'; from Siena to Pisa for another tourist was 'the whole way a most pleasant and delightful garden'.[25]

Verbal testimony could be infinitely multiplied, and the visual evidence, too, is extensive. Paul Brill, one of whose landscapes Kent purchased in 1714,[26] had drawn an Italian villa, its garden and adjacent farming land to illustrate the series of months. What is interesting about two of his sketches in the Louvre is that they clearly show how a villa garden thrusts itself out to dominate the surrounding fields. Similarly, the engravings of the Tuscan countryside which Giuseppe Zocchi issued in 1744 declare the same interpenetration of gardens and worked land. This last is often 'poeticised' with arcadian figures resting on tombs, but it is also actively managed by farm workers and serviced by commercial wagons and rivercraft.[27] It is perhaps this same half-poetical vision of the countryside that Kent engineered at Rousham by transforming a distant cottage into the Temple of the Mill, and by introducing farm carts into his landscape drawings (see cat. no. 12 and 13).

The word *villa* had passed from Latin into Italian and was absorbed into English during the seventeenth century, not without some comment on its especial usefulness to designate a country estate where house, garden and countryside were interconnected. When English visitors to Italy first saw villas on what had been classical ground they also noticed their proximity to farmed land or to *vigne*. This Italian word, meaning vineyard, if it did not lead to any etymological confusions with *villa*, did nonetheless suggest actual and topographical coincidences of country houses with agriculture which classical authors had first suggested. So when Warcupp's substantial guidebook called the Orti Farnesiani on the Palatine Hill 'nothing but ruins and the vineyard of Cardinal Farnese' or when in the 1720s Wright, proceeding down the Via Flaminia into Rome, recorded his impression of 'good Buildings, pleasant villas and Vineyards on each hand', the close connections – if not the confusions – of villa and vigna were established.[28] Behind it all lay the weighty

12 Giuseppe Zocchi, Villa La Tana, drawing, early 1740s (?), Pierpont Morgan Library

authority of the younger Pliny whose letters describe how his villas were set in a various landscape of hills, woods, fields, vineyards, meadows and cornfields. It is precisely this classical precedent that the early Augustan landscapists like Stephen Switzer and Alexander Pope invoke. The former cites Virgil in his *Ichnographia Rustica* of 1718 to support his plea for 'rural and extensive Gardening' and this Roman tradition surely sustains Pope's famous claim that the garden must 'call in the country'. As his drawings endlessly imply, Kent's garden work grew out of this same context of classically derived garden tradition, mediated and authorised by modern Italian examples.

The English interest in the mixture of what Spence called 'country and gardens' has already introduced the second aspect of Italian gardens that concerns this study of Kent: its variety. For the siting of villas in the midst of rural landscapes necessarily made the vistas into that countryside a distinctive part of the experience of gardens that were also considered to be full of excellent diversity. The whole idea of *variety* much preoccupied Europe in the late sixteenth, the seventeenth and the early eighteenth centuries. The roots of such an interest may be traced to Aristotle's *Rhetoric*, which notes how the human mind delights in change, and to the Christian recognition of God's essential goodness and optimism which fathered 'unoutspeakable riches'. Often, though, an attention to variety, at least in the late seventeenth century and in Kent's time, did not entail any reference whatsoever to larger theories which argued reasons for a human inclination towards variety. Variety was pleasant in and for itself.[29]

Throughout the seventeenth century Italian gardens had been commended for their variety. Indeed, it became a *sine qua non* of a fine garden: Veryard is quite specific that the Villa D'Este gardens at Tivoli are superior to any either in Italy or the whole world by reason of their 'greater Variety of Rarities'.[30] It is praise of the great variety of waterworks in the villas at Frascati, especially Villa Aldobrandini (13), of which Kent was evidently fond, that underpins almost every written account of them. In his *Elements of Architecture* Sir Henry Wotton had praised some 'incomparable' Italian garden for its 'diversities' and 'various entertainments'.[31] Such remarks echo throughout the literature of travel and garden design between 1624 and the decade of Kent's stay in Rome. Nor is it only, as we might expect, mannerist and baroque gardens that elicited commendations of variety; in smaller, less obviously diversified designs visitors felt that they experienced this essential quality. Thus the Medici villa of Castello Fynes Moryson had found 'full of pleasant hills', while Sir John Reresby was delighted by the 'great variety' of plants and design elements at the Giusti Gardens in Verona.[32] Any garden that was situated on a hillside augmented its variety with what Wotton called 'mountings and valings'. Small and large gardens invoked this characteristic criss-cross structure of stairs and ramps which allowed architects to establish gardens on sloping sites. The influential model of Bramante's Belvedere Courtyard, which first used this structure and had itself taken the scheme from the ancient temple complex at Praeneste, allowed architects to establish complex gardens on sloping sites. Kent would be able to invoke this in one commission at Rousham, otherwise his reliance on Italian variety manifests itself rather in a tendency to concentrate upon local moments within larger estates, highlighting specific items rather than focusing on overall patterns, and in his clear delight in prospects. Italian hill sites allowed views out into the countryside, and for later travellers these prospects are more and more valued. Since Rome was built on seven hills its gardens invariably delighted with 'incomparable prospect'; but Joseph Spence was struck by this when he visited, as Kent had done some years earlier, the Medici estate of Poggio a Caiano.

Another mode of variety to please later tourists like Addison or Spence who were associated with the English landscape garden and its 'calling in of the country' was the division of gardens into regular and irregular or 'natural' areas. This, too, had the *imprimatur* of the younger Pliny. Exactly what Pliny's piece of rural imitation looked like we cannot know; Burlington's protégé Robert Castell had one stab at a reconstruction. But the Italian Renaissance garden, in both conscious and less deliberate emulation of Pliny, had involved wilder parts in the garden *ensemble*. Popular representations (14) of the Villa Lante in Bagnaia showed the geometrical garden and its lodges alongside a far less organised wood into which the iconography of the garden was nevertheless extended.[33] The Villa Farnese at Caprarola, where several English visitors recorded a visit, had not only its two rectangular gardens immediately adjacent to the fortress-like house but a beautiful casino retreat in the woods reached by a path through the meadows. Other Italian gardens engineered what in 1752 John Northall called 'spots free from artificial improvements, where nature displays its beauties'.[34] They were certainly just as contrived as the remainder of the layout, but contrived in a different, rural style. One of the more interesting examples was the Villa Doria Pamphili in Rome, where one traveller specifically distinguished between its gardens and 'many large walks in and about the Park'.[35]

13 Gaspar van Wittel, called Vanvitelli, *Fountains in the Villa Aldobrandini, Frascati*, drawing, 1713 (?), Trustees of the Chatsworth Settlement

14 Anonymous, *The Villa Lante, Bagnaia*, painting, seventeenth century, Collection Sir Harold Acton

Perhaps because of this careful juxtaposition of regular and irregular the Villa Doria Pamphili came to play an interesting but hitherto unnoticed role in the new gardening movement in England. For when Batty Langley came to issue his *New Principles of Gardening* in 1728 he used as his frontispiece an engraving of the view down that tree-lined water course at the Pamphili which connects garden and park; except that he changed the baroque fountain at its termination into a quasi-gothic ruin, thereby signalling the translation of an Italian idea into an English idiom.[36]

Kent's drawings show that he responded specifically to these aspects of Italian garden variety. He seems to have known the Doria Pamphili gardens and even perhaps Giovanni Giacomo de Rossi's book of engravings of them published in the late seventeenth century;[37] that he would not have known Langley's book seems impossible, especially in the light of its frequent references to Italian garden design. By the time Langley published the *New Principles* and Kent was beginning some of his garden work the invocation of variety as a specific English need – in contradistinction to the French love of uniformity – was routine. Actually, the French garden did not by any means lack variety: among the bosquets and compartments of Versailles and Marly the experience of diversity and surprise would have been just as striking as at Tivoli. But it had become *de rigueur* to think of the French as more precise than various in their expressions: thus Dryden contrasted the 'barrenness of French plots' to the 'variety and copiousness of the English'.[38] His plots are those of drama, but the same distinction was made about garden plots, and in seeking to oppose French styles in gardening as in drama it was to Italy, both classical and

Renaissance, that the early eighteenth century looked. The long tradition of praising the variety of Italian garden styles found its final justification in the endorsement of English landscape diversity.

Theatres and gardens

We may take up the third important aspect of an Englishman's Italian garden experience, its theatrical quality, by considering Kent's involvement in theatre designs. That links were thought to exist between garden and theatre designs is demonstrated by Kent's drawing in the Soane Museum (cat. no. 70). This seems to be the representation of some scene from a pastoral play or (more likely) opera, where two characters, a satyr and a shepherdess, act out their exchange upon a stage with descending levels and against a backdrop which shows the hermitage that Kent designed for the gardens at Stowe; the only addition is the name ARCADIA inscribed above its central arch. What this Soane drawing suggests is that Kent could clearly think of his garden work and his stage designs as interchangeable. Dating is impossible, but establishing the chronology would not undermine the point that designing scenery in landscapes and contriving scenery for the theatre were for Kent ineluctably connected.

We need to consider several aspects of this topic: the enthusiasm of his patron, Burlington, for theatrical enterprises, Kent's own work for the theatre in Rome and London and the connections established in Italy between gardens and theatres.

We know how involved Burlington's family was in promoting Italianate opera in England.[39] His contacts (in England, in Italy while on the Grand Tour, and in England again after his return) with designers like Filippo Juvarra are signalled in part by the large number of theatre designs which he collected and of which Cinzia Sicca has counted eighty-nine at Chatsworth. In the Devonshire Collections besides there is an album (dated about 1729) of theatrical *capricci* by Juvarra which the artist presented to Burlington.[40] In Italy Burlington clearly maintained his operatic and theatrical interests and had contacts with Cardinal Ottoboni, another promoter of opera, for whose private theatre Juvarra acted as scene designer until 1713 and with whom Kent also had dealings.[41]

Kent's own involvement presumably began in Rome. Details are sparse, but one particular incident which he must have witnessed is hugely suggestive. His companion, John Talman, designed an extraordinary entertainment for the Academy of Virtuosi in 1711 to celebrate the feast of the patron saint of painters, St Luke. In letters to his father Talman describes his work for this event at enthusiastic length:

> I had an entertainment wc. is ye talk of y whole town . . . I had y best musick in Rome composed on purpose . . . & commending Several persons yre. present who were all y top Virtuosi in Rome both for Learning & arts; there was y Chief Painter, Architect, Sculptor, Medalist &c in Rome w: some of y most eminent persons for learning, y Prince of y Academy was my Lord Cornbury . . . y room was full of Scenes illuminated & hung w: festones of myrtle & flowers, round y room were 12 heads painted representing Vitruvius, Fabius y Painter, Glycon y Sculptor; on y

opp: side were Palladio, Rafael & Bonarota, on an other side Inigo Jones [Isaac]
Fuller & [Edward] Pierce. at y upper part Horace y Poet, Rossius y Comedian &
Ismenia a Singer, w: abundance of motto's in Latin & Italian . . .

Talman toasted Queen Anne, somebody read a four hundred line poem 'in praise of Arts'
and this was followed by a 'Symphony of musick & singing', after which everybody
retired to a cypress grove, where a further illuminated picture 'representing all y Arts' was
displayed.[42] In subsequent letters Talman hoped that he would be able to repeat the event
on an even more lavish scale; he never did so, but what he achieved once is enough to
make us realise how much Kent existed in a society where elaborate and allegorical
divertimenti maintained the traditions of Renaissance entertainment. A vital English
chapter of that tradition was known to the Burlington circle through the collection of Inigo
Jones masque designs.[43]

Kent clearly continued this mode of courtly entertainment once he returned to England.
Lord Hervey reported that at a masquerade in December 1731 Frederick, Prince of Wales,
appeared as a shepherd attended by eighteen huntsmen 'dressed after a drawing of Kent's,
in green waistcoats, leopard-skins and quivers at their backs . . . tragedy buskins upon
their legs . . . antique gloves with pikes up to their elbows, and caps and feathers upon
their heads like a Harry the 8th by Holbein'.[44] These specifications are very similar to the
masquing designs by Inigo Jones for the Jacobean and Caroline courts; the combination of
classical and Tudor effects, as we shall see,[45] was a hallmark of Kent's garden designs.

Otherwise, the dearth of information on Kent's theatrical contributions is frustrating.
We know that he provided settings and costumes for a production at the Theatre Royal in
Drury Lane in 1724, which is only five years after his return from Italy. He is credited also
with the sets for Niccolo Porpora's semi-operatic cantata, *Il Festa d'Imeneo*, in 1736.[46]
Besides the Soane drawing of a pastoral opera (cat. no. 70), at least one other theatrical
subject by Kent survives: in the Ashmolean Museum (15) there is a drawing which shows a
fantastic drama in progress within a proscenium arch, a giant addressing a lady in a
Kentian rendition and mixture of Serlio's tragic and comic stages.[47]

It is perhaps safe to assume that this theatrical, masquerade and entertainment activity
of Kent's which has come down to us is but the tip of the iceberg (the scarcity of theatre
designs not being so surprising when one thinks of how they would be spoiled in
carpenters' and scene painters' hands). It seems likely, therefore, that some of his
surviving landscape drawings may be preliminary designs for the theatre. In a bound
volume of Lord Burlington's theatre designs at Chatsworth is a rough, very faint drawing
that is undoubtedly Kent's (cat. no. 47); but if it had not been found in that context, it
would doubtless have been taken for a landscape sketch with clear affinities to others at
Chatsworth. It therefore provokes the question whether some of those other drawings
which we have supposed to be of or for actual landscapes are not in fact theatre designs,
either drafts of backdrops or sketches for whole scenes like that in the Soane Museum (see
for example cat. no. 31). Such a question is sharpened by the connections between theatre
and garden that existed in Italy and which Kent would certainly have known.

The story of the development of what we now recognise as traditional theatre architecture is complicated and need not concern us. But one element of it is crucial: the fashion
in which gardens were invoked as a *luogo teatrale* or *lieu théâtral* during and after the

15 William Kent, drawing of stage
action, Ashmolean Museum, Oxford

Renaissance.[48] The climate of Italy urged outdoor performances, and princely gardens
offered themselves as ideal settings. And from being adapted for occasional use, gardens
came to include theatres among their various architectural features. Indeed, a variety of
theatrical shapes and structures could be discovered throughout gardens in later periods,
whether or not such spaces were used for performances, and even whole gardens came to
be shaped in theatrical form. Grottoes, too, often presented dramas, sometimes figures
moving to the sound of music, all hydraulically operated.[49] Some of the most visited in
Italy were those of the Medici villa at Pratolino which Kent singled out in the diary of his

1714 Italian tour (2); he noted particularly 'Galatea coming out of her Grotto drawn by Dolfini'. Kent's phrase is closely linked to the language of dumb show, masque scenario or stage direction, a pattern that was frequent in travel accounts of Englishmen on the Grand Tour and revealed their appreciation of the links between gardens and theatres.[50]

When entertainments moved inside into specially provided theatres more or less as we know them, the connection with gardens was not lost. Since so much of the repertoire of these entertainments, especially the *dramma per musica*, involved pastoral and/or mythological themes, gardens featured prominently in their imagery; a garden was a *locus amoenus*, a privileged location where the mysterious working of art found its ideal stage, as Talman's scenario in Rome makes perfectly clear.

Kent's knowledge of these Italian connections between theatre and garden determines, as will be shown, some of his most characteristic landscape sketches and designs. He is especially fond of establishing in both large areas (Holkham, Euston) and in smaller, secluded spots (see cat. no. 61) versions of an amphitheatre. In these exedral clearings he presents his spectators with the opportunities to be both spectators of a garden's dramas or even to participate in them. This double response, so fundamental to the English experience of Italian baroque gardens,[51] seems to have been translated and naturalised in English landscapes by William Kent. Some of his drawings imply that he envisaged these English garden stages or scenes as locations of various kinds of play: social play, the play of fantasy, the play even of a historical imagination. The landscape or scenery in these drawings often seems to be but the appropriate background for humans and/or historical-mythological personages; it is even sometimes as if Kent was less interested in the formal shapes and lines of a landscape for their own sakes. And where his sketches are empty of 'action', we should recall that the scenes he was designing would be filled by human visitors or actors, exactly as he shows them in cat. nos 18 and 62.

But it would have been difficult for such a theatrical perspective not to have melded with his thinking and practice as a history painter. Both the contemporary theatre and history painting shared a concern with human action, with devising scenery or ornaments that would be appropriate for that action, with an appeal to classical texts, with a repertoire of gestures in which the visual matched the verbal, with an organisation of space within picture or proscenium frame that obeyed conventional principles of perspective.[52] So to appreciate the full implications of his theatrical designs for gardens we must turn to his work as a history painter and the related designs for illustrated books.

'Ut pictura poesis' and garden pictures

One of Kent's patrons while he was in Rome, Burrell Massingberd, hoped that his protégé would become a *Raphael Secundus*.[53] Kent himself recorded how his companion for part of the time in Italy, John Talman, was 'continually preaching to me that I may be a great painter'.[54] To be a great painter, a second Raphael, meant above all a commitment to subject, to the representation of significant action and story. This is exactly what Kent did when he painted St Julian the Hospitaller for the ceiling of the Flemish church in Rome, S. Giuliano dei Flamminghi, or sent back a panel for Chicheley Hall depicting *Mercury watching Herse and her sisters before the Temple of Minerva*. Such history painting clearly shared with the theatre the centrality of some significant subject matter. In his easel painting of *The Return of the Prodigal Son*, Kent may have given much more prominence to its architectural setting than he did, for example, in his *Jupiter and Semele* at Kensington Palace or *The Banquet of the Gods* in Burlington House, but the fine prospect of gardens and grandiloquent buildings speak of the wealthy world of family and household to which the prodigal returns. And in the other paintings which we know Kent did it was evident that subject matter always predominated: in Rome he was working on paintings of Homeric subjects – Agamemnon sending to Achilles for Briseis ('a subject', the artist noted, 'never before done') or 'Venus a-conducting Helina to Paris'.[55]

At this point it will be useful to set both Kent's work for the theatre and his other activities as a painter, which can usefully be related to his work as landscape designer, in a wider context of ideas and forms: the visual languages that were available to painters and to theatre artists and to illustrators such as Kent himself in the first half of the eighteenth century. Much of this has come to shelter under the convenient but often misleading umbrella of *ut pictura poesis*. Horace's casual phrase has accommodated a wide range of ideas which do not easily declare themselves at the utterance of that Latin tag; so some enquiry is required into the possibilities which this idea of the parallels between the arts could include, as well as some attention to how the whole idea of what was apt for a picture (and therefore 'picturesque') was changing during Kent's lifetime. Since his landscape work has so readily been hailed as picturesque, it is above all essential to ask how Kent himself viewed the picture in the first place before he invoked it as a model for landscape compositions.

Pope's use of the term *picturesque* is a useful place to start. It has little to do with the later enthusiasms of Gilpin, Price and Knight at the end of the eighteenth century: for Pope it is a French term and means picture-like, and while it may include landscape features it does not refer to them solely. Pope instances his understanding of the term with a couplet by Ambrose Philips: 'All hid in snow, in bright confusion lie,/ And with one dazzling waste fatigue the eye'. Obviously such a scene cannot be a picturesque landscape, even by a Dutch painter like Avercamp who specialised in winter scenes: Philips's landscape simply has no variety. What for Pope is clearly picturesque about it is that it is an apt setting for the writer of an epistle which is entitled *To the Earl of Dorset from Copenhagen*.[56]

Pope has two rather more substantial uses of the same term in the commentary to his translations of Homer, which Kent would have known since he provided various illustrations and decorations for *The Odyssey*. These references to picturesque emphasise the whole ensemble of a scene which is envisaged as a painting executed by an artist who would 'rien omettre des circonstances nécessaires dans la composition d'une histoire'.[57] Twice Pope draws his readers' attention to Homer's composition of an *histoire*. The first occasion is in the context of the night piece in Book VIII of *The Iliad*, which is distinguished by the 'liveliness of its paintings' in which the 'prospect' is the 'chief Beauty'. But this landscape has as its *raison d'être* the figures of Rhesus and Dolon and the Thracian forces.[58] This subservience of the setting to its human subject is even clearer in a note to Book XVI:

We see Patroclus touch'd with the deepest Compassion for the Misfortune of the *Greeks*, [whom the Trojans had forc'd to retreat to their Ships, and which Ships were on the Point of Burning] prostrating himself before the vessel of *Achilles*, and pouring out his Tears at his Feet. *Achilles*, struck with the Grief of his Friend, demands the Cause of it. *Patroclus*, pointing to the Ships, where the Flames already began to rise, tells him he is harder than the Rocks or Sea which lay in prospect before them, if he is not touch'd with so moving a Spectacle, and can see in cold Blood his Friends perishing before his Eyes. As nothing can be more natural and affecting than the Speech of *Patroclus*, so nothing is more lively and Picturesque than the Attitude he is here describ'd in.[59]

We are invited to read the Homer passage as if it were a painting by Raphael, perhaps, or Nicolas Poussin or Le Brun, and in that painting to see the rocky shore and the burning ships, excitingly rendered by this 'poet-painter', as a visual simile for Achilles's obduracy and his friend's passion, an equivalence to which Patroclus's gesture draws attention. If Homer's had indeed been a picture in the grand style of late seventeenth-century taste it would undoubtedly have alluded to a literary text as Kent's paintings from *The Iliad* did, knowledge of which texts would explain the scene. The visual simile too would be translated into words ('harder than the Rocks'), and the gestures – what has been termed the legible body[60] – of the actors were equally amenable to verbal elucidation. All of this is a far remove from the later opinion of Wordsworth whom Farington records as arguing that 'Historical subjects shd. never be introduced into Landscape but when the Landscape was to be subservient to them – Where the Landscape was intended principally to impress the mind, figures, other than such as are general . . . are injurious to the effect'.[61]

It seems that Kent's work as a landscapist is too often seen from that Wordsworthian perspective and not enough in the light of theory and practice contemporary with him. His friend Pope's concept of beauty in a picture requires the cooperation of theme and form. Kent's paintings have often the air of a similar subscription to those academic rules. Formal presentation, whether drawing or colour, light and shade, or perspective, are all to be contrived in the interests of the central subject, which Dryden (translating French academic theory for his countrymen) saw as some significant and unified human action. And Pope knew Dryden's 'Parallel of Poetry and Painting', for it was reissued in 1718 with his own *Epistle to Jervas*, a painter who travelled with Burlington to Italy in 1714.[62]

However, it is too simple to see Kent as an artist in bond to academic principles. Those same principles were being challenged, and the period with which we are concerned saw the beginnings of a fundamental realignment of priorities whereby the order of *inventio*, *dispositio* and *elecutio* was reversed.[63] These changes originated in France and percolated somewhat unsystematically into England. Briefly, the new approaches shifted the emphasis in painting from the subject and its contrivance to the form and the handling. Dryden himself acknowledges the choice when in his lines *To Sir Godfrey Kneller* he distinguishes between the Venetian and the Roman schools of painters; 'One colour'd best, and one did best design./ Raphael's, like Homer's was the Nobler part;/ But Titian's Painting, look'd like Virgil's Art'.[64] The options that Dryden suggests without committing himself to one or the other were to be fully expounded by the Abbé du Bos in 1719 and made available in an English translation by Thomas Nugent in 1748, the year of Kent's death. The older tradition the Abbé called 'Poetic composition', the newer and more radical one, 'Picturesque composition'. The older one, as we have seen, urged a principal and unified action in a painting and had clear literary authority, while its challenger allowed painters to give primacy to colour and merely formal effects. And subject matter is barely mentioned in this second, so that literary allusions to narrative texts or to explication of the passions displayed are also suppressed.[65]

Old and new attitudes towards a picture could exist side by side. Jonathan Richardson urges the viewer of Raphael's cartoons to invent dialogue for the figures represented, which would bring out the centrality of event and human passions. But he could also, analysing Poussin's *Tancred and Erminia*, insist that its story – an exact instant in which narrative the painter has captured and where he has admirably visualised expressions – is nevertheless secondary to the 'harmony' of the piece which derives primarily from its colours: 'without considering it as a Story, or the Imitation of any thing in Nature the *Tout-ensemble* of the Colours is a Beautiful, and Delightful Object'.

It seems to me that Kent's *oeuvre* must be situated in the very centre of these opposing principles. John Gay, another intimate of the Burlington circle, appears to be saying just this when he applauds Kent's painting in his 'Epistle to Paul Methuen':[66] Raphael is said to 'live again' in Kent's designs as well as 'Titian's strong fire and Guido's softer grace', thereby invoking both the masters of subject painting (Raphael) and of colour and 'picturesque' effect (Titian and Reni). The situation in which Kent found himself after his return from Italy must have highlighted the alternatives: on the one hand, he was encouraged to believe that he had the makings of a great history painter (what Gay claims, unless there is some ironic undertow), and that great history painters are what England needed;[67] on the other, his own talents lay rather in those designs for silverware, furniture, gardens, even some architecture where the formal play of shapes, lines and masses could predominate. In terms of contemporary aesthetics he was far more accomplished in picturesque composition than in poetic invention. With hindsight we can readily see Kent's place in these magnetic fields of theory and taste, and generally we have opted to interpret his career in progressive, teleological ways, whereby the *outcome* of aesthetic debates is allowed to explain the interim stages.[68] We should, however, recognise Kent's situation at a watershed, looking backwards to theories and practices that he knew well and also moving slowly forward towards ideas and forms that he could not have known would prosper as in fact they did. This means that as far as his landscape designs are concerned he would be compelled by the centrality of some human subject or history as well as by the opportunities for merely formal effects. But the pull of the older views was for him still a strong one, and here his work and partiality for the theatre and the illustration of literary texts lent their authority. For in drama, obviously, the human story is still central and subservient to the scenery; while the events Kent chose to illustrate from literary texts almost always revolve, similarly, around some significant action.

Relatively early in his career, in 1720, soon after his return from Italy, he illustrated John Gay's *Fables*. The four frontispieces for James Thomson's *The Seasons* come in 1730. The far more numerous designs for Edmund Spenser's *The Faerie Queene* come at the end of his career and are posthumously published. We may explain the greater prominence of landscape in these final designs and the relative absence of landscape in the Gay ones by

W. Kent inv et del.   n. Tardieu Sculp.   16

W. Kent invet del.   n. Tardieu Sculp.   17

Kent's own involvement with garden design in the interim. Also, of course, Spenser pays far more attention to landscape than do Gay's *Fables*. But even in the Spenser work Kent always keeps the landscape subservient to the central action; while in the four designs for Thomson he very carefully follows the poet's own emphases upon the human experience of landscape which *The Seasons* make the basis of a larger philosophical enquiry.

   The four frontispieces for James Thomson's *The Seasons* appeared in the quarto edition of 1730 (16–19). In an octavo edition the same year the illustrations used were engravings of four statues of the seasons in the garden at Versailles. The difference between these two illustrated texts could not be more marked. In one, emblematic images which the reader identifies and translates into verbal form ('spring', 'summer', etc.); in the other, a varied scene in which supernatural and human figures inhabit a landscape appropriate to them and their seasonal tasks. At the top of each design Kent still invokes allegorical language common to the Versailles statues or baroque ceilings, but it is dominated by a more expressive imagery of rural landscape. Furthermore, while one set of plates is of French

16 Tardieu after William Kent, titlepage for Thomson's 'Spring', 1730

17 Tardieu after William Kent, titlepage for Thomson's 'Summer', 1730

18 Tardieu after William Kent, titlepage for Thomson's 'Autumn', 1730

19 Tardieu after William Kent, titlepage for Thomson's 'Winter', 1730

origin, Kent's is more Italianate and (if we accept Kenneth Woodbridge's interesting suggestion that they are influenced by frescoes in Veneto villas)[69] Palladian as well.

All four designs observe certain decorums. Human figures occupy a central position, though in Winter they are less dominant – a visual acknowledgement of the season's inimicable climate. The human figures echo the postures of the zodiacal deities, sometimes by common imagery (sickles in Autumn), sometimes by shared or answering gesture (the peasant in the bottom right of Winter flinching from the threatening judgement of the god on the storm cloud; the repertoire of benign hand and arm positions in Summer's bathing nymphs and sky-borne divinities). Moreover, these dominant representations of human action influenced by seasonal forces which the superior figures emblematise are provided with landscapes that are – as Pope had argued a few years before about Homer's 'pictures' – apt for the central drama. In Spring, for instance, the rainbow is echoed in the lake, and its intimation of new beginnings answers the expectant gesture of the shepherd immediately below it, two pairs of lovers and the skipping lambs.

The fidelity of Kent's designs to Thomson's poems is of less concern here than the fact that human action finds its appropriate setting. Certainly Kent seems to have wanted to honour Thomson's text, since he emended the group of bathers in Summer in 1744 to accord with the poet's revision of the Musidora passage.[70] Equally he translated into visual forms the poet's philosophical emphasis on man's apprehension of his place in a larger world: here the eloquent prospects, views deep into landscape, suggest the huge territory of nature, which the poet frequently invokes and links to metaphysical themes; and the rich variety of landscape, where our eye is invited to seek out and explore, parallels Thomson's insistence upon man's necessary alertness to the scope and meaning of the natural world around him. But although these and some more ingenious correspondences between the poetry and Kent's designs have been proposed by critics,[71] all we know about Kent's literacy does not suggest that the point to make about these plates for *The Seasons* is the artist's intelligent and scrupulous translation of text into image. Not that kind of *ut pictura poesis*. Rather, Kent clearly shares with Thomson certain attitudes towards both significant human action as the subject matter of art and the languages available for its representation: the *ut pictura poesis*, then, of Dryden's 'Parallel of Poetry and Painting'.

The Thomson designs also foreground another concern relevant to Kent's landscape work. This is the conscious 'translation' of classical motifs into English contexts. The frontispieces show a mixture of classical and contemporary: naked figures of nymphs (one of whom echoes the Medici Venus), bucolic shepherds out of Claude Lorrain's and others' classicising pastorals; but also hunting parties in modern dress, English farmland and indigenous trees. Mediating between this antique and modern imagery are neo-palladian buildings of the sort that Burlington was promoting in England, just as Palladio himself had translated the study of antique baths and other ruins into architecture for the estates of his Venetian patrons.

The designs for *The Faerie Queene* were done at the very end of Kent's life and published posthumously in Thomas Birch's edition of 1751. Their claim on the attention of garden historians has generally been based on a reported remark of Kent himself that 'his taste in gardening [was caught] from reading the picturesque descriptions of Spenser'.[72] But William Mason, who recorded that 'frequent' claim of Kent, went on to note, somewhat caustically, that 'However this may be, the designs which he made for the works of that poet are an incontestable proof that they had no effect upon his executive powers as a painter'. Yet Mason's judgement on Kent's abilities as painter must not distract us from asking what relationships may exist between the Spenser designs and Kent's landscapes.

As has often been noticed, two of the Spenser plates depict buildings that Kent had designed for the gardens at Stowe: Archimago's cell is a version of the Hermitage (cat. no. 73), while Phedria's island in Idle Lake (cat. no. 78) is graced with a palladian vision, the Temple of Venus from Stowe (with possibly, further up the hillside, Rousham's Praeneste Terrace). Other details could be related to Kent's gardenist interests: the nymph Diana changed into a fountain (cat. no. 77) is an Ovidian motif familiar to Kent from his visits to Italian gardens;[73] while occasional buildings, both neo-classical and gothick, appear as they do in his sketches for country house landscapes. But such slight parallels do not seem the crucial aspect of a relationship between Spenser's poem and Kent's work as a landscape designer. If Kent did indeed say frequently that his taste in gardening was caught from reading the picturesque passages of *The Faerie Queene*, we must recall what his friend, Pope, had argued about the picturesque in another poet, Homer: namely, that the Greek poet's skill lay in writing words which could provide a history painter with the materials for a scene in which human action, detailed and narrative, was set in a landscape that answered the needs of that central event. Pope may even have been the person who not only alerted Kent to the picturesque possibilities of writers but first introduced his friend to the delights of Spenser, whom we know he admired prodigiously.[74] And Pope is also on record as approving the remark of an old lady that *The Faerie Queene* was 'a collection of pictures'. Since old ladies of 'between seventy and eighty' may be expected to have conservative ideas, this one's judgement of Spenser tallies with what we know of Kent's painterly taste and Pope's endorsement of what constitutes 'picturesque'. So if we are to read anything into Kent's linking of his landscape designs with his reading of Spenser, it should be *The Faerie Queene*'s collection of scenes in which some central action is located with all due decorum in appropriate landscape.

That as late in his career as the 1740s Kent should focus so firmly upon human action rather than landscape pure and simple in his Spenser illustrations is something which proponents of his advanced and progressive gardening, 'picturesque' in a teleological sense, have never adequately faced; just as they have never coped with Kent's earlier delight in Italian gardens like Pratolino. Of course, landscape functions centrally in the Spenser illustrations, just as it does in *The Faerie Queene*, although it should be noted that there are important aspects of Spenser's descriptions, their moral implications, which a visual artist could not easily translate, even if he spotted them and wished to do so. Thus Phedria's 'cunning little nest' in Spenser's phrase becomes simply a Kentian prospect with a typical joke of putting two of his own designs on the island as an 'example of the best'.[75] Nor can the hypocrisy of subtle Archimago's hermitage be conveyed visually. But Kent does give to his landscapes a sense of surprise and hidden, to-be-discovered, recesses and distances. This, whether consciously derived from Spenser or not, parallels the poet's demand of the alert reader to question where a landscape leads and what are the moral consequences of a particular description. We can also learn about Kent's attitudes towards these Spenser scenes from his preparatory drawings, many of which survive. When they were engraved they simply bore an identifying caption and a cross-reference to the page where the illustrated action occurs.[76] In this way they focus upon a specific narrative moment (unlike the Thomson plates which aim to give a unified idea of a whole season). The drawings are even more specific, anchoring the visual event with extensive verbal tags: *dramatis personae* are labelled, items of scenery named, and brief hints of the action indicated by phrases somewhat close to stage directions (see cat. no. 74).

It can perhaps now be seen that very similar assumptions underlie Kent's work as a history painter, illustrator, and stage designer: not only the primacy of subject over treatment, but the range of emblematic and expressive gesture, the strong obligations of visual to verbal. It is hard to believe that when Kent's energies turned to garden and park design he simply abandoned all those assumptions about thematic and formal requirements. It may even be that when his attempts at history painting after his return to England aroused so much hostility and hilarity[77] and he was diverted into other enterprises he nevertheless maintained some of the central concerns of an art in which it had always been his ambition to succeed.

But there were inevitably problems inherent in transposing into landscape gardening theories and practices derived from painting and theatre. The media were, to start with, strikingly dissimilar, though what was common to them all was the need for perspective which Kent studied (as perhaps would any painter) while in Italy.[78] How is two-dimensional, illusionary and background scenery in a painting to be translated into what is real, three-dimensional and central on some country estate? Theatre scenery would mix three-dimensional sets and painted backdrops, but it still used human actors to represent the story. In a garden, the responsibility for an equivalent 'action' rests primarily upon its temples, statues, inscriptions and other such devices and then upon its visitors who explore and 'read' its scenes but are not a permanent part of them. To see how Kent came to solve some of these problems of translating strategies from his other work into his enthusiasm for gardens it will be necessary to look at his designs in this, for him, new art form.

2 'The pencil of his imagination'

It was an essential part of Walpole's encomium on Kent's landscape designs that he was 'painter enough' to 'bestow … all the arts of landscape on the scenes he handled'.[1] In other words, Walpole ascribes to Kent's training as a painter the formal solutions – 'perspective, and light and shade' – which in his opinion characterised Kent's landscaping. Insufficient of Kent's paintings survive to support (or, alternatively, none ever existed that could support) this contention. But we are fortunate that many drawings of garden and landscape subjects do survive, and in these we may examine more carefully Walpole's claims for 'the pencil of his imagination'. First, it will be useful to categorise and describe them, before beginning to deduce from them what may be called an 'identikit' of the Kentian landscape. Roughly one third of these garden and landscape drawings survive in the Devonshire Collections at Chatsworth, having gone there from Kent's chief patron, Lord Burlington. The remainder are scattered, but at least half of these are to be found at the places for which the designs were intended – Rousham in Oxfordshire, Euston in Suffolk, or Holkham in Norfolk.

The scope of surviving drawings

As the catalogue at the end of this volume clearly reveals, Kent's work in this field ranges from highly finished drawings to either faint pencil drafts or what amount to doodles. John Wilton-Ely has noted that many of Kent's drawings reveal a 'certain lack of coherent perspective and frequent disparity of scale' which 'might well suggest a need to express or resolve ideas swiftly rather than reflecting any artistic incompetence'.[2] Many also reveal the exuberant, even zany humour, sometimes via distortions or caricature, that was clearly a hallmark of Kent's personality. A similar stylistic declaration of temperament may also be recognised in the evident speed of his drawing, the reliance on rapidly stroked trees of two rudimentary shapes (either bushy or the characteristic Kent spruces, sometimes like a child's Christmas tree) and in the inclusion of some human or animal, especially canine, activity which undermines the solemnity of a scene.

But by far the most important aspect of Kent's drawing style is the change which appears to have come over it around 1725, a change which John Harris has recently suggested may derive from Kent's admiration for Claude Lorrain's *Liber Veritatis*.[3] This record of his paintings executed in pen and wash came to London sometime after 1720 and was available for Kent to study in the library of Devonshire House, just down Piccadilly from where Kent was lodged in Burlington House. Its characteristic style had no precedent in English drawing, including what little of Kent's early work has survived (Harris instances the sketch for the ceiling of San Giuliano in Rome) or what we may deduce of his drawing from the frontispiece engraved after Kent's design for Gay's 1720 *Poems on Several Occasions*. Yet from the mid 1720s Kent's own preferred mode of drawing was in black ink, washing the outlines in yellowish-brown. The influence, then, of Claude upon Kent's drawing style is highly probable; but the significance is not limited just to formal matters. Kent's interest in that style may also be seen as an attention to Claude's dedication to history painting with a strong, often arcadian, landscape element just at the time when Kent's own landscape interests were beginning to develop.

In general, we may identify six kinds of landscape or garden drawing, each of which is worth considering separately.

The first category is finished drawings which may presumably be presentation gifts – that of Pope's garden (cat. no. 66) is clearly not a proposal for a garden since we know it was already established; given its fanciful staffage and its portraits of Pope, Kent and Pope's dog, it could well be a record and tribute of friendship. The various scenes in the Chiswick gardens of his chief patron, including those of the entrance to the villa (cat. nos 23 and 24) are also likely to be homages to Burlington's prize creation. That of the Vale of Venus at Rousham (cat. no. 105) could also be a presentation drawing; alternatively, as with that for the Chatsworth hillside (cat. no. 18), the Rousham view was finished in order to show patrons what the achieved scenery would represent. Since there are other drafts of this Chatsworth hillside (cat. nos 16 and 17 among others), it is probable that Kent worked up only those designs which sufficiently commended themselves and so were worth the effort. Such might be the case with cat. no. 26, a view of the cascade at Chiswick with a boat on the water below it and a carriage departing, a vision created once the final disposition of the cascade itself had been determined.

A second category consists of more or less complete scenes, yet without the polished rendition of Pope's garden or the Vale of Venus. Cat. no. 13 is a good example of this mode – the scene as a whole is depicted, but the pen and wash has been rapidly put into the larger elements of the scene. As has already been suggested, some of this kind of work, including cat. no. 13 itself, could just as well be versions of theatre settings – either backdrops or preliminary impressions of a set. But drawings that are clearly proposals for country estates – at Euston, for example, Claremont or two views of a deer park – are attempts to convey the impression of extensive areas of ground where architectural features, even if substantial structures, are absorbed into the large landscape.

A third category of sketches is for precisely those individual architectural items; these sketches, sometimes quite elaborate, concern structures presumably to be placed in a larger landscape that was not Kent's concern; what he usually does is provide them with some hint of a setting. These hints can be very rudimentary (cat. no. 64), somewhat wing-like and theatrical (cat. no. 67), or simply with typical Kentian spruces brushed in so as to signal a landscape context. Some of these could be drawings of existing buildings rather than projections for new structures, but it is likely, as with the various designs for the Chiswick cascade, that this category consists largely of projections.

Surprisingly less than half a dozen drawings either contain instructions for their execution or present plans alongside elevations as one might expect in architectural proposals. Only one drawing has survived with directions for workers on the site (cat. no. 60), and even that might conceivably be notes by Kent to himself. This absence of instructional drawings may, of course, be explained by the fact that any papers used on site by gardeners are likely to be in no state for retention,[4] just as theatre designs, once sent into the workshops, would be virtually destroyed by carpenters and scene painters. It is clear, at least from the documentation we have about Rousham,[5] that Kent, having in some form communicated various garden scenes, expected them to be realised by local work-men on the spot, to whom fell the sometimes worrying task of determining how to translate his pictures or other directions into objects on the ground. The few garden and landscape sketches with plans as well as elevations are perhaps more surprising given Kent's career as an architect. But what is arguably the first design Kent ever penned for a garden building (cat. no. 59) took the form of a ground plan without any elevation. The others we have suggest that he drew plans either to organise his thinking about a new project – the Richmond Hermitage sheet (cat. no. 57) – or on occasion to pass on to workmen (cat. nos 90–92). Otherwise he worked as Walpole claimed that he did, like a painter; this training, together with his experience in the theatre, meant that he usually envisaged designs in terms of their appearance from one fixed vantage point.

Another distinct group are spontaneous or casual sketches, even rapid doodles, the occasion of which might have been either idle fantasising or, since they often enough have some clearly humorous tone, the product of some high-spirited social occasion of which we catch glimpses in Kent's correspondence.[6] These are not necessarily related to design proposals, though cat. no. 6 may be; rather, they seem to use existing locations – the Chiswick aviary (cat. no. 14) – as a setting for some amusing incident or personal reference.

The final two categories are *capricci* and drawings intended for engravers. Not all of the former are landscapes, but that Kent turned frequently to what John Wilton-Ely has reminded us was a traditional vehicle for artistic experiments must suggest that he viewed actual landscapes as potential territories for fantastic collocations.[7] This is clearly true of the most finished *capriccio* (cat. no. 46), which involves various memories of Kent's Italian experience. Some drawings which would fit other categories in this survey are also clearly modes of *capriccio*: the view in Pope's garden (cat. no. 66) or the landscape with a version of Euston, a river god and large dog (cat. no. 6). And, as will be argued later, Kent's fundamental instinct as a landscapist was to devise a *capriccio*, a collection of reminiscences and allusions to many other sites: the most finished version of the Chatsworth hillside (cat. no. 18) does precisely that, as in a much larger format does the whole *ensemble* at Rousham.

Finally, drawings, some quite finished, that were intended for the engraver are essential to any assessment of Kent's landscape designs; the majority of the interesting ones in this category are for Spenser's *The Faerie Queene*, a text which will be seen to play a significant role in the early English landscape movement.

The most conspicuous absence from this corpus of drawings are, as has been noted, plans: even where we might expect plans or maps to have been drawn up – the large territories where Kent was called upon, like the grounds at Badminton or the parks at Esher and Euston. In fact, there are only two surviving sheets which constitute any exception to Kent's apparently habitual practice of thinking in pictorial, perspectival terms. One is a frustratingly faint proposal for Badminton which takes the form of a large bird's eye view (cat. no. 5) – the closest Kent comes to mapping. The second, recently discovered, is a roughly sketched plan of a flower garden beside the River Mole at Esher: doubtless the organisation of flower beds and the disposition of what may be sunken studs (buried containers of plants) required him to think in this format; but his characteristic instinct to see things as in painting reasserts itself at the top of the sheet where he draws a boat-house in elevation and beside it, though for a space he continues to show a bridge and stream in plan format, he sketches one of his favourite belts of trees to show how their trunks would provide an open colonnade along the bank (cat. no. 94).

Another, perhaps less surprising fact is that there are so few designs for gardens in the proximity of houses where it might be expected that much more regular layouts would be in order: in fact, the drawing for Claremont (cat. no. 60) proposes to remove Vanbrugh's terrace in front of the 'great room'. There are, it is true, designs for Badminton and Holkham which suggest geometrical layouts; but the views of terraces, ascending and descending stairs, with the ornaments of vase and statue, that have been assumed to be Kent's work and are collected at Chatsworth along with his other drawings are clearly *not* from his hand.[8] That they were thought to be so at some point is, however, of some interest if we are to locate his landscape work in its proper historical context.

The drawings in the light of other evidence

What can this body of Kent drawings tell us about his work? Can we invoke them to fill out hints about his practice from other sources? George Vertue, for example, writes of 'Mr Kent at Court and amongst people of quality, call'd on for drafts &c on all occasions'. Kent himself seems to have been eager to provide patrons with all sorts of designs: he offered the Earl of Huntingdon assistance with furniture – 'if I can be of any service, I shall always be ready to give my advice'.[9] So we may assume that he found himself suggesting ideas for parks and gardens as well as for furniture and other interior decorations. The drawings endorse this account of his gardenist career. Kent obviously sidled into garden and landscape designs from his commissions in other fields. Partly this was a consequence of his promotion by Burlington: once his history painting proved less than acceptable,[10] Kent's evident versatility was readily deployed in Burlington's political campaign to dominate the aesthetic scene. So it was that Kent was taken on by the Prince of Wales to design the gardens at Carlton House in 1732 or was commissioned by Queen Caroline to provide buildings for Richmond Park.

Another aspect of Kent's work as a garden and landscape designer which the surviving corpus of drawings suggests and other data confirm is that apart from Esher – begun in the late 1720s and finished a decade later – and the later projects for Euston, Holkham and Badminton, he was called upon to re-work estates already designed by others (such as Vanbrugh's and Bridgeman's Claremont or Bridgeman's Rousham) or he was invited only to suggest items for already existing layouts. That would also perhaps explain the absence of any plans. In all of his sketches for specific, local additions or reworkings in larger estates he is clearly concerned to provide for their immediate surroundings: even the briefest of scribbles for the Richmond Hermitage (cat. no. 57) sets out its appropriate ensemble. That this habit may derive from the nature of his commissions cannot be ignored; but it is also typical of a stage designer's role – see, for instance, the specifically theatrical setting of the Arcadian hermitage in the Soane Museum (cat. no. 70). It is, however, also characteristic of the viewpoint and format of a painter.

All eighteenth-century analyses of Kent's landscape work agree in seeing it as painterly. Spence records that 'Mr Pope and Kent were the first that practiced painting in gardening ... [but] Kent had little more than the idea of mixing lighter and darker greens in a pleasing manner'.[11] Walpole in his turn claimed that the 'great principles on which [Kent] worked were perspective, and light and shade ... Thus ... he realized the compositions of the greatest masters in painting'.[12] Such testimony is borne out by Kent's sketches, which usually take the eye backwards into the imaginary field of vision, an illusion created and enhanced by perspective and chiaroscuro.

In what are presumably some of Kent's last drawings, the illustrations for *The Faerie Queene*, these effects are called up to effect a structure that is also often adopted in the specific landscape designs, namely recession, whereby the eye is tempted into the imagined scene, just as the feet, following the call of the eye, would be on actual sites. Such scenery with a built-in invitation to explore its only hinted-at features has various origins. One is clearly the practice of landscape painting. But a painter's invitation to explore the depicted space is always illusionary, whereas two other art forms, the garden and theatre, authorised and realised actual movement. Kent was familiar enough with Italian gardens, where generations of English travellers had commented upon the opportunities afforded their eyes and feet: Wotton's passage in *Elements of Architecture*, cited earlier,[13] is one such testimony. The other source, itself probably derived (at least in part) from those Italian gardens, is the moving scenery of Inigo Jones's masques, which by *its* alterations allowed stationary spectators the illusion that *they* were exploring the spaces unfolded onstage. Yet this illusion was partly realised at a masque's end when members of an audience mingled in a dance with the actors. This dimension of the masque would have been recoverable both from published masque texts, with their often elaborate stage directions which attend to the effects upon spectators, and from the surviving designs by Inigo Jones which Kent would have known in Burlington's collection.

Some examples will be useful. In *Oberon*, performed in January 1611, Jones presented the audience first with 'a dark rock with trees beyond it and all wildness that could be presented' (this is similar to Kent's presentation of some of his set pieces of garden scenery). Later in the masque the 'whole scene opened, and within was discovered the frontispiece of a bright and glorious palace'; later still, the interior rooms were disclosed, but 'in perspective' (i.e. painted on backcloths). Such an experience, incidentally, is almost exactly the reverse of that which visitors experience in the Boboli Gardens, Florence, as they move towards the façade of Buontalenti's Grotto: first they see an architectural 'frontispiece'; then, as they move closer, this dissolves into natural rockwork along the top of the pediment and inside the first room.[14]

As the designs for *Oberon* and other masques clearly indicate, backdrops or 'perspectives' were also expected to elicit an audience's imaginative reading of their flat surfaces; Kent, for whom the authority of Inigo Jones in the Burlington circle was second to none but Palladio himself, could clearly have read these designs in a similar way and, with his knowledge of analogous experiences in Italian gardens, have translated the effect into three-dimensional garden forms. Faced with the backdrop for *Coelum Britannicum*, for example, members of an audience could have imagined themselves in just such a garden as Wotton described, where from a high terrace a general view of the gardens below could be taken before a visitor was 'conveyed again by *mountings* and *valings*' through the garden.[15] Or consider the following stage direction from that same masque as a parallel experience to Wotton's 'incomparable' Italian garden:

> the scene again is varied into a new and pleasant prospect clean differing from all the other, the nearest part showing a delicious garden with several walks and parterres set around with low trees, and on the sides against these walks were fountains and grots, and in the furthest part a palace from whence went high walks upon arches, and above them open terraces planted with cypress trees …[16]

It is this sense of movement through garden spaces that was translated into Kent's sketches and illustrations of less regular sites and, apparently, into the actual layouts that were realised from his suggestions, as this account of his work at Claremont reveals:

> The walk to the cottage though destitute of many natural advantages and eminent for none … is yet the finest part of the garden; for a grove is there planted, in a gently curved direction, all along the side of the hill, and on the edge of a wood, which rises above it … The intervals winding here like a glade, and widening there into broader openings, differ in extent, in figure, and direction; but all the groups, the lines, and the intervals are collected together into large general clumps, each of which is at the same time both compact and free, identical and various. The whole is a place wherein to tarry with secure delight or saunter with perpetual amusement.[17]

As these remarks from 1770 indicate, Kent's painterly and theatrical handling of space was susceptible to interpretation in progressive ways that satisfied a later taste. Yet it was equally indebted, we can be sure, to Kent's experience of older Italian gardens.

This ambiguity, this potential for both atavistic and proleptic analyses of Kent's work, is rarely acknowledged; yet it lies at the root of any attempt to determine his place in English gardening history.

One of the famous contemporary statements on the progressive aspect of Kent's work is Sir Thomas Robinson's letter of 23 December 1734, addressed to the Earl of Carlisle:

> There is a new taste in gardening just arisen, which has been practised with so great success at the Prince's garden in Town [Carlton House], that a general alteration of some of the most considerable gardens in the kingdom is begun, after Mr Kent's notion of gardening, viz., to lay them out, and work without either level or line. By this means I really think the 12 acres the Prince's garden consists of, is more diversified and of greater variety than anything of that compass I ever saw; and this method gardening is the more agreeable, as when finished, it has the appearance of beautiful nature, and without being told, one would imagine art had no part in the finishing, and is, according to what one hears of the Chinese, entirely after their models for works of this nature, where they never plant straight lines or make regular designs. The celebrated gardens of Claremont, Chiswick, and Stowe are now full of labourers, to modernize the expensive works finished in them, even since everyone's memory. If this grows a fashion, t'will be happy for tht class of people, as they will run no risk of having time lay on their hands.[18]

The Prince of Wales had acquired Carlton House from Lord Burlington in 1732 and had asked him to modernise it; presumably Burlington promoted his protégé for the gardens. Exactly what part of Kent's design actually fitted Robinson's remark about 'without either line or level' is unclear, partly because the grounds have disappeared. We know that at right angles to the house Kent built a domed neo-palladian temple (perhaps cat. no. 67), which enjoyed a vista down the length of the gardens. At the midway point was a large circular flower-bed, surrounded by an arbour.[19] The arbour was open on two sides to allow a vista (20) down which the visitor was tempted beyond the flowers to discover a regular pool in irregular groves at the end of the garden (a familiar Kent combination, though usually the pool is irregular too). Only in this final section could the lack of geometrical planning (no 'line' or 'level') have been apparent. If, however, Robinson's quite categorical remark refers to the whole garden, then the only possible explanation is that he was translating into surveyors' language his impression of a garden which swung the visitor round on the garden front of the house, then led him through

20 Carlton House Gardens, engraving by Woollett, 1760

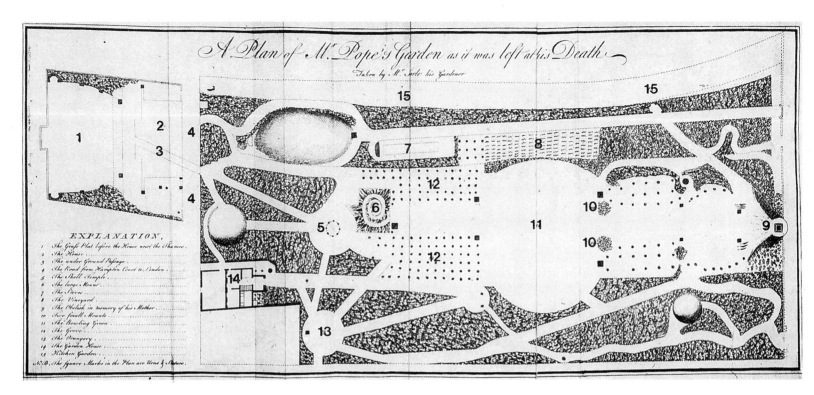

21 Plan of Pope's garden at
Twickenham, drawn and engraved by
J. Serle, 1745

opening and closing spaces down the lawns and arbour and groves into the irregular climax which thus coloured his sense of the whole.

Such an effect had already been established by Pope in his garden at Twickenham,[20] which Kent would certainly have known, and it is possible that Carlton House echoes and elaborates it. Straight lines are eliminated around the edges of the Twickenham garden,[21] while the main axis, though eventually straight, begins with a kink and thereafter is characterised by what Walpole called 'retiring and again assembling shades'. Perhaps Kent learnt this manipulation of spaces along one axis from Pope's Twickenham;[22] yet it was also a feature he could have learnt at first hand from both Italian gardens and the illusions of theatre settings.

What has never been asked of Robinson's description is exactly whose judgement is being recorded in the phrase following 'viz.' – his own extrapolation or an off-the-cuff boast by Kent himself? The phrase may simply refer to what appears to be Kent's practice not to provide plans and surveys for his garden designs or a deliberate decision not to use the established tools of the gardener, and therefore be Kent's own explanation of his method or even an exasperated remark Robinson picked up from workmen engaged upon transforming the site with only pictorial sketches to go on. Furthermore, the style of many sketches suggests that Kent evolved his ideas in rapid pencil strokes, faintly at first and only confirmed later if at all in pen and wash, a technique sufficient in itself to promote the notion of Kent's working without line and level.

Kent's habitual invocations of geometry are difficult to adjudicate. One sketch survives with directions to *remove* the line of a terrace immediately in view of the house (cat. no.

60). Yet a few other drawings do contain straight lines or levels: cat. nos 22 and 52 are attempts to maintain geometry in relation to buildings; cat. nos 1 and 21 rework existing sites without removing their original geometry. (The only drawings at Chatsworth which do make a feature of terraces and other regular garden features are not, it will be recalled, by Kent.) Otherwise Kent's designs are for features set in parkland which would not have necessitated 'level or line'.

Obviously we must give considerable weight to Robinson's testimony, but the kind of garden work in which Kent was engaged – piecemeal designs to modernise existing sites – and the evidence of his working habits which the surviving drawings imply, go some way to explain it.

Gardens as classical history paintings

This fascination with Kent's formal attitudes towards his landscape pictures, however, neglects another, to which Robinson's mention of 'beautiful nature' and 'variety' gestures. This is the idea that gardens were paintings of a more traditional kind, namely history or mythological paintings, in which concerns for *la belle nature* and variety were traditional. Whether Robinson simply ignores these or takes them for granted (probably the latter) cannot be determined. The comments by Spence and Walpole on Kent's painterly habits already quoted seem to ignore them completely; but both were writing some time after Kent's death and were much determined by the rapid advance of aesthetic theory from poetic to pictorial composition, discussed in the previous chapter. They thus neglect the pull of older theory and traditions of painting upon Kent, for whom those painterly devices of perspective and chiaroscuro were means of focusing attention on some central action. Similarly, but more obviously, Kent's theatrical designs would also have functioned to contain and shape a dramatic action. Spence's indication that Kent had a relatively slight appreciation of picturesque techniques in his gardening in fact implies that he failed to grasp this dimension of Kent's painterly approach.

We can gain some insight into this painterly organisation of garden space as a means of foregrounding 'action' if we attend anew to Pope's remark, reported by Spence himself, about his own garden design: 'You distance things by darkening them and by narrowing the plantation more and more toward the end, in the same manner as they do in painting, as 'tis executed in the little cypress walk to that obelisk'. For Pope in 1739 the painterly organisation of his grounds was completed by the installation of the monument to his mother which thereby promoted the centrality and 'readability' of human action in the little cypress grove at its end.[21]

Yet the central problem here, as has already been noted, concerns the transposition of painterly practice into gardens and, specifically, how to observe propriety and decorum – in other words, which themes and styles were appropriate for English history painting in gardens? Kent's puzzlement over Pope's 'allegorical' obelisk ('Pope in a mourning gown with a strange view of ye garden to shew yt obelisk as in memory to his mothers death, the alligory seem'd odde to me …') maybe suggests his own difficulties with this matter of translating into garden scenery the action of stage and history painting.[22]

First, it will be helpful to consider a typical neo-classical statement about action in history painting. John Dryden had raised this issue as far as it concerned English art when he considered the traditional theme of a painter's *inventio*:

> The composition of the painter should be conformable to the texts of ancient authors, to the customs, and the times. And this is exactly the same in Poetry: Homer and Virgil are to be our guides in the Epic; Sophocles and Euripides in Tragedy: in all things we are to imitate the customs and times of those persons and things which we represent …[23]

… *ut pictura poesis*. But what of *ut pictura hortus*? What were the ancient texts to give authority to modern garden work? And what indeed were apt compositions of persons and things for gentlemen's seats in Hanoverian England? It was, of course, a theme which exercised literary and artistic minds in Augustan England – Hogarth adapting history painting or Fielding the epic to modern purposes in *The Harlot's Progress* or *Tom Jones*; Pope first translating Homer and later imitating Horace. It seems useful to suggest these, if not as an influence upon Kent's own solutions in adapting history painting and Italianate garden design to English use, at least as the appropriate context.

Pope himself touched upon the problem in 1713. While Kent was still in Italy Pope published in *The Guardian* his translation of some lines from Homer describing the garden of Alcinous: he introduced it with the comment that it constituted 'the most beautiful Plan of this sort that can be imagined'.[24] It is an odd remark, since the passage which follows can hardly be said to provide or even yield a plan; but it suggests that Pope at this date looked to the classics even for his garden ideas. At that stage, however, he had yet not embarked upon any of his own gardening. Nor had he set himself to do more than translate Homer into English, to make him 'speak good *English*'.[25] He was later to move from translating Homer to imitating Horace, a subtle change of tactic that implies his concern to adapt the classics for his own times and his determination to make Horace behave linguistically as if the classical poet were writing in, for and about contemporary England. The gardenist equivalent of these concerns with translating classical culture into English was to find for Vitruvius, Pliny and other classical advocates of villa life some appropriate English dress. It was the ambition of the Burlington circle to accommodate Palladio in England just as he had translated classical forms into modern buildings for his Venetian clients. This is surely the context in which Kent's own garden work, like Pope's, should be interpreted. The Kentian garden is the translation into modern English of traditions of Italian gardening (ancient and modern). Another of Burlington's protégés, Robert Castell, obviously more scholarly than Kent ever was, read Pliny's gardening texts in the light of modern, English ideas. Kent's garden designs should, then, be seen as part of Burlington's larger enterprise of answering Shaftesbury's call for a new national taste in the arts. This will explain the phenomenon, often puzzling to modern commentators,[26] of neo-palladian buildings set down in natural landscape, since both were an attempt to recover the purity of ancient styles and naturalise them in England.

On his return from Italy Kent found the Dutch and French taste of England, from which he had been absent almost ten years, quite unacceptable: 'I am afraid by what I hear that our gusto is still in the little Dutch way'; as late as 1766 John Gwynn explained that Kent was 'the first who ventured to attack and cut up the Dutch mince-pies of Bridgeman', a judgement that Spence echoed once he had encountered Dutch gardens in 1737.[27] Soon after he had returned to England in 1719 Kent humorously declared that 'an Italian constitution' like his found the winter climate of 'this Gothick country' unsupportable and that his only consolation was going to Italianate 'Operas'.[28] It is all something of a jest and a pose, but Kent fancied himself as Italianate. And operating within Burlington's circle he could readily indulge that taste and its corollary, a distaste for Dutch and French things.

Kent's designs are full of an Italian-ness, a *color romanus*. At Chatsworth his various suggestions for how the hillside could be treated invoke a variety of antique and modern Italian imagery. The most finished of them (cat. no. 18) alludes to the Temple of Vesta at Tivoli, to Roman pyramids and to the rustic cascades of the Villa Aldobrandini at Frascati, a town famous precisely for recreating in modern splendour the lost glories of antique Tusculum's country retreats.[29] Setting these features into the Derbyshire hillside offers an approximation of a history painting: the figures which usually distinguish Kent's finished drawings are in fact spectators of Kent's transformation of antique gardens, mediated by Italian Renaissance examples, on to English soil. Yet by their acknowledgment of his inspiration and achievement they are also participants in this moment of cultural history.

But as Pope's neo-Augustanism must remind us, the translation of classical culture into Georgian England was by no means uncomplicated. A satiric alertness to discrepancies between the meanings of Horace's villa and his own at Twickenham, especially between their respective attitudes to the city, sustains much of Pope's imitation of the Roman poet. Earlier in his career he transposed a version of Sarpedon's speech from *The Iliad* into the mouth of Clarissa in *The Rape of the Lock*, wittily identifying (for those who noticed) the declensions between the two societies thereby compared and contrasted. Something of this scepticism is borrowed by Kent for his various representations of Pope upon his own ground (cat. no. 66). But his most obvious identification of a similarly satirical juxtaposition of classical and modern is to be read in the Elysian Fields at Stowe. It seems to be generally agreed now that Kent's contribution was to design the buildings, and that the overall iconographical programme was the responsibility of Cobham and his friends.[30] There seems no reason to dispute that, though there is a case for one new proposal for a possible contribution from Kent. All we know of Kent's personality would suggest that he was a willing participant in the whole enterprise and that he would have learnt from it.

The Temple of Ancient Virtue at Stowe (8) was modelled by Kent on his (and indeed others') preferred classical Temple of Vesta at Tivoli, though with some glances both at other similar edifices and at the Mausoleum at Castle Howard, the first English imitation of this Roman temple style. The Stowe building therefore incorporates an allusion to the history of a particular building form. But it is also juxtaposed via the painterly device of perspective to three other buildings: to the gothic of Stowe parish church, to a Temple of Modern Virtue, deliberately built as a ruin and graced (if that is the word) with a headless statue supposedly representing Sir Robert Walpole, and to Kent's other building here, the Temple of British Worthies (22 and cat. no. 109). It is especially the juxtaposition of Ancient Virtue and British Worthies that concerns us, though the latter's mixture of styles, half classical and half gothic (its squat pediments and ancient British figures) announces a theme which will be examined in detail later.

22 The Temple of British Worthies, Stowe (*photo: R. & H. Chapman*)

23 Detail of engraved view of the Villa Mattei, Rome, from Falda, *Li Giardini di Roma*, 1683

24 Detail of engraved view of the Villa D'Este, Tivoli, from Jean Blaeu, *Théâtre de l'Italie* (1704)

Did Kent recall another occasion in Rome when ancient and modern were satirically compared? Did he perhaps recount to the Cobham circle at Stowe Talman's entertainment which we have already discussed? Talman tells us that his designs for that Roman divertissement included 'yt temple of Virtue (wch I represent in a Scene)', a vista along a cypress walk with a representation of all the arts that incorporated twelve painted heads including those of Vitruvius, Palladio and Inigo Jones, and finally a picture of the Liberal Arts 'in a melancholy posture'.[31] The Stowe scenario is more subtle, but nonetheless curiously similar. Ancient Virtue is a reconstituted Roman ruin, inside which were displayed four full-length statues of Greek worthies; across the little valley the British Worthies are both more numerous (does it take more to compete with antiquity?) and only represented by busts.

The Temple of British Worthies itself is a curious mixture of classical reminiscences, modern Italian designs and a vaguely indigenous squatness. Kent had considered using a version of the design at Chiswick (cat. no. 34), so its classical credentials must have been established. Yet Kent manages to imbue its appearance at Stowe with his own characteristically sceptical gloss. Its shape has been attributed by Kenneth Woodbridge to the exedra in the Villa Mattei in Rome (23); that would be a significant allusion, since the gardens of the Villa Mattei were a Renaissance recreation of a classical funerary garden and their echo at Stowe in the Elysian Fields would be aptly elegiac.[32] But there are other candidates for such an exedral shape in many other Italian gardens such as Villa Borghese and Villa D'Este (24). The exedral shape in itself, moreover, declared both an antique and a modern Roman inspiration all the more powerful for being generalised; it signalled a wide variety of classical ruins and the imitation of their forms in Renaissance gardens. But unlike the models already cited, Kent's curved temple at Stowe has a feature which incorporates a typical Kentian joke: on the rear is a tribute to one, Signior Fido, apparently a gentleman

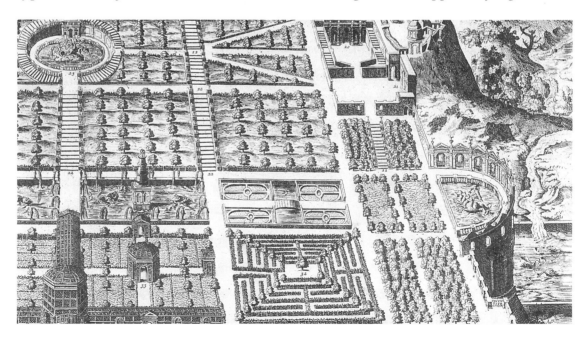

25 Roman busts in niches at the Villa Brenzone, Lake Garda (*photo: author*)

whose exemplary virtues are all listed; except that the punch line shows Fido to have been not an Italian but an English hound. Even British Worth succumbs to a cheeky put-down, similar to all those other Kentian dogs disporting themselves and doing other doggy things among the classical scenes of gardens like Chiswick (see cat. no. 30). Here, too, there is a possible Italian source: the beautiful circle of niches with busts of Roman emperors at the Villa Brenzone on Lake Garda, which are all hollowed out in the rear (25); these empty spaces have a rather disconcerting effect, somehow undercutting the firmness and the graceful circle in just the way that Signior Fido pre-empts the British Worthies. Whatever the detailed allusions that Kent employs, the point is clearly that his play with classical references and their aptness for this English scene is part of a thematic as well as a formal design.

   Of course, by no means are all classicising features in Kent's designs to be read as having this sceptical sense of their relevance to the history painting of English garden scenes; tone and content are exceptionally difficult to identify without some context. It is, however, clear that Kent's drawings are distinguished by a high proportion of items whose inspiration is either classical or classical via Italian Renaissance models. Temples in groves are a particular feature, and it is perhaps no accident that Kent's contemporary, William Stukeley, singled them out as a particularly ancient feature of landscape design.[33] Kent himself would have found that his Italian exposure to this phenomenon was further endorsed by Burlington's own practice at Chiswick, where the garden vistas (as Rocque's engraving of 1736 shows) were all terminated by classical temples or – since the miniaturisation of antique models signals their accommodation to an English site[34] – tempiettos. Kent clearly loves the sense of discovery which the situation of buildings behind an open screen of trees imparts to a viewer or visitor; visual penetration is achieved while keeping the effect of enclosure, but what the eye sees may tempt the feet to explore. Jacques Carré has suggested that this feature (see, for example, cat. no. 34) derives from Kent's fascination with Palladio's intercolumnation at the churches of the Redentore and San Giorgio Maggiore in Venice[35] – an important reminder that garden design did not look exclusively to other gardens for inspiration.

Temples in groves, dense or open, are not Kent's only classicising 'speciality'. So, too, is the dotting of statues in woodland, clearly a reminiscence of many Italian gardens where antique or modern statuary was placed in irregular as well as regular garden spaces.[36] Urns please him also, doubtless for the formal play of shapes – rotundity contrasted with the lack of such strictly artificial shapes in nature – though they would also recall distinctive Roman effects like the terrace arrangements of the Villas Borghese or Doria Pamphili in Rome. River gods, as already suggested, have a particularly strong classical resonance, and were also much invoked in gardens. Kent's classical repertoire further includes obelisks and arches, actually found at Chiswick, but suggested for other patrons at Euston and Holkham. Then there is his evident delight in exedral shapes of all sizes, echoing both Roman ruins unconnected with gardens and their use in modern gardens. Even his frequent designs for cascades, deriving in part from the need to supply such a feature at the head of the serpentine river at Chiswick, recall those on the rustic hillside at Frascati's Villa Aldobrandini. In short, to leaf through Kent's designs is quickly to register both his delight in an eclectic anthology of Italianate items relocated either in the groves which were a distinctive feature of Renaissance gardens or in more open settings reminiscent of the Roman Campagna and his use of this imagery for its allusive potential.

'This Gothick country'

But this *color romanus* of many of Kent's garden and landscape designs is not the whole story. What of his *gothick* work? Indeed, despite his (maybe mock) distaste for 'this Gothick country' soon after his return from a warm and classical Italy, he seems to have been eager and inventive with gothick work. His first architectural commissions for gothick were at Hampton Court, where he rebuilt the east range of the Clock Court, and at Esher;[37] in both, as John Harris has noted, Kent was extending and modifying existing

Tudor buildings. Harris has also noted that this gothick work of Kent's is 'an associational style, not a revivalistic one'.[38] So we may legitimately ask, then, what were its associations.

It is possible (and tempting) to think that even gothick was, for Kent, Italianate. His friend, John Talman, had provided some drawings for the remodelling of the hall and chapel of All Soul's College in 1708, just before he and Kent went off to Italy.[39] Talman already knew Italy, and he annotated his proposals for All Soul's with 'unlike any other in Oxon & pretty much after ye Italian Gothick'. It is also likely, as Harris argues, that Kent would learn about Italian gothic from Talman while on their travels, notably at Milan Cathedral. But unfortunately we cannot take the matter much further. Yet in the heart of Palladio country in 1714 Kent applauded the 'very much Gotic' of St Mark's, Venice.[40] So it is possible that Kent saw gothic, too, as a style that linked Italy and England and could therefore be invoked in his campaign to contrive a suitable decorum in garden history pictures. Gothic that was both Italian and English could also signal a progress of the arts, a topic to which we must now turn. For gothic was what Vitruvius or Palladio might have 'spoken' if he were British.

Here an important drawing in the British Museum (cat. no. 62) is illuminating. The drawing shows at the left Hampton Court, where Kent had worked, and the extended front of Esher in the distant right. Between them on a hill is a version of one of his neo-palladian pavilions set in a grove. This spectacle of Tudor/gothic and classical landscape is watched by a couple in the foreground on the banks of a river, down which a triton drives his sea-horses. In the margins of the drawing are verses which, according to Kent's recent biographer, 'seem to show that Kent was attempting to write a poem'.[41] In fact, these verses have been copied by Kent from Michael Drayton's famous topographical poem, *Poly-Olbion*. Written between 1613 and 1622 (a period not insignificantly marked by the beginnings of Inigo Jones's work), this consists of thirty 'Songs' on the beauties of the English countryside. Drayton explains his work as 'A Chorographicall Description of Tracts, Rivers, Mountains, Forests, and other Parts of this renowned Isle of Great Britaine, With intermixture of the most Remarkable Stories, Antiquities Wonders, Rarityes, Pleasures and Commodities of the same'. His main focus is upon rivers and streams, here – in the lines that attracted Kent – the rivers Thames and Mole. The title, *Poly-Olbion*, means 'having many blessings', and its significance for the poem is clear; its Greek derivation alerts us also to the theme of the 'progress of the arts' whereby England was seen as ultimately succeeding to the glories of the ancients, transferred across the ages and finally across the continent of Europe to the British Isles.[42]

This is exactly the message that underlies so much English gardening in the first fifty years of the eighteenth century, and it goes far to explain the nonchalant mixture of classical and gothick styles in gardens like Stowe or Rousham and in much of Kent's own designs including those for Esher where he toyed with a classical before settling finally for a gothick house (cat. no. 81). To locate in the English countryside buildings in either style was to declare, not just aesthetic taste and preference, a delight in merely formal opportunities, but, as George Clarke and Michel Baridon have argued, quite precise cultural and political ideas.[43] We need to locate Kent's work in these contexts.

At least since the Glorious Revolution of 1688 the theory of a limited monarchy had been closely affiliated with the political thought of the ancients, mediated by a modern

Italian thinker like Machiavelli whose ideas were popularised in England by Harrington and later Toland. Their arguments for a mixed monarchy claimed as model the Roman pattern of consuls (=Monarch), patricians (=Lords), and *comitiae* (=Commons). As it was put in *Liberty* by a poet with whom Kent was associated, James Thomson: 'matchless constitution, mixed/Of mutual checking and supporting powers,/King, lords and commons'. In such a political vision, the revival of classical architecture in England becomes eloquent of a larger political geography, as London (in Toland's words) became 'a new Rome in the West' and 'could grasp at empire like Rome itself'.

But in this vision of the classical relevance of republican Rome, what possible place could be found for gothic fabrics? To quote Baridon, it seems surprising 'at the same time [to] celebrate the Roman empire and those who destroyed it'.

Part of the answer to that question is to be found in another strand of cultural history. In 1718, the year before Kent returned from Italy, the Society of Antiquaries was re-founded, and under the presidency of William Stukeley did much to promote the study of English ruins. That Kent would have been well aware of its activities may be assumed from his correspondence, whilst in Italy, with Samuel Gale, who became the Society's first treasurer. Under the fresh scrutiny of the antiquarians and in the context of political justifications of 1688 English ruins could be cherished for their own sakes. For if the aristocracy needed to be seen as guardians of public liberties, then as wielders of such influence in mixed government their own ancestry had to be stressed; there was no better way to do so than to champion the antiquities of their landscape, a land from which their power derived. Indeed, the ruins of monasteries around England was often a specific sign of the beginnings of landed power for families who received church lands from Henry VIII. There were historical precedents, too, for associating a modern English political settlement with its non-Roman past: both Magna Carta and King Alfred, the founding father of a system of civic liberty lost at the Norman invasion, sustained the myth of gothic freedom, which in its turn was imaged in eighteenth-century gardens by Bathurst's restoration of the so-called Alfred's Hall at Cirencester or Cobham's triangular gothick Temple of Liberty at Stowe.

In short, we may see at precisely the time Kent began his garden work a doubleness of response to the past and its architectural styles which did not imply any contradiction.[44] To celebrate republican Rome with classical buildings tallied with the recognition of a native gothic past, because both were intricately involved with Britain's major claim to contemporary political fame: the Glorious Revolution of 1688. A political associate of Lord Cobham's, Temple Stanyan, wrote in the dedication of his *Grecian History* that ancient virtue 'was a noble vigour, with which [the Greeks] were animated against the first disturbers of mankind; and it is that makes [the moderns] naturally have recourse to those, who have so gloriously exerted themselves in securing the liberties of Europe'.[45] In such contexts it is useful to set such a sketch as Kent's of Claremont (cat. no. 63), which shows a classical pavilion against a screen of trees above which rises Vanbrugh's gothick belvedere, exactly capturing this double regard. This is not to argue that Kent deliberately utilised the two styles with conscious political meaning, but that such ideas and assumptions lay beneath the surface and sustained his, and others' work. It is impossible to ascribe everything simply to 'taste', for taste must have its basis in larger structures. Kent's drawing of Hampton Court and Esher, with its classical deities on the English river and the palladian building on a distant hill above a Tudor Esher, clearly does declare (as Drayton's poem on the English heritage with a Greek title had done one hundred years before) the happy conjunction of antique, Italian and gothic styles in England's political geography and their meaning in its cultural history. With hindsight, we can of course see that Kent's gothick interests would blossom into the Gothic Revival, but that is yet another teleological ambush for the historian. Like Kent's 'picturesque' designs,[46] his use of both gothick and classical styles in gardens places him at a crossroads: we should not try to run him out of town in one particular direction signposted Strawberry Hill, Grasmere, Gilpin or Gainsborough.

The role of the garden visitor

Perhaps we can now see more clearly how Kent's so-called picturesque taste in garden design is affiliated to his play with both classical and gothick styles, usually considered simply as formal languages. As a painter turned landscapist he sought to frame in garden scenes some significant action along the lines of history painting. His fascination with classical and gothick styles of building which his drawings continually declare was also a concern with two political versions of English history, not contradictory but complementary. Thus, when Joseph Spence reported that the Elysian Fields at Stowe were 'the painting part' of Cobham's gardens,[47] he was perhaps responding to the inherent 'action' to which Kent had contributed: different forms of architecture with different associations and meanings confront each other and are established in various perspectival vistas interpreted by the alert visitor, the participant in, as well as spectator of, this scene.

The Elysian Fields constitute indeed the history painting part of Cobham's gardens. And they also make clear how pictures were susceptible of translation into garden scenes. In the first place, the garden scenes 'represent' action and ideas – ancient virtue, British worth – as any history painting did with its painted figures, and to do so they also utilised the perspectival illusion of painting (or the actual perspective of theatre sets). Secondly, the garden visitor registered this representation by his or her keen response to architecture, sculpture and inscription; these various elements constitute the text or script of a representation. But by involving him/herself in such an activity within the garden, unlike the spectator always outside the picture space or proscenium arch, such a visitor also became a protagonist, for this representation of cultural history has meaning only by virtue of its reception by a contemporary in the very midst of the 'action'.

This double role of the garden visitor can be gauged best from Rigaud's drawings of Chiswick and Stowe.[26] They give prominence to the humans who seek to understand what they contemplate, showing them thereby involved as actors in the garden scenes, even giving them gestures familiar to contemporaries from dramatic practice and history painting.[48] Indeed, Rigaud can make explicit what is only implied in verbal descriptions. John Macky's guidebook, for example, says that at Chiswick 'Every walk terminates with some little Building, one with a Heathan Temple, for instance the Pantheon, another with a

26 Jacques Rigaud, detail of Gibbs's Building, Stowe, drawing, 1733–34, Metropolitan Museum of Art, Harris Brisbane Dick Fund 1942

little villa …'.[49] Macky there notes what may be seen, but Rigaud shows the very acts of observation – which Kent also does in some of his more finished drawings.

Rigaud also reveals that not all visitors are as actively engaged as others, which is consistent, too, with both drama and painting in which some event will involve central participants, some interested witnesses and some casual, even oblivious bystanders. A parallel may also be drawn between these various involvements in reading a garden and the kinds of attention which a writer like Pope expected from readers of his *Dunciad*. A dunce or Grub Street hack could presumably not participate in the poem's fullest ironies as could, say, the Lords Cobham and Burlington. Indeed, that is precisely what the poem is in part about – registering parallels between contemporary poetry and its heroic traditions involves the privileged reader in its moral-political-literary action where the quality of his response constitutes a vital part of that theme. If Kent was at all influenced by Pope, then it is this stress upon the spectator's ability to appreciate his role in a scene, an emphasis implicitly made in many of his drawings, that may have been among the best fruits of that friendship.

But the intellectual emphasis in such learned 'history painting' as the gardens of Stowe or Chiswick is by no means the whole story. We have seen Robinson, Spence and Walpole all ignore its demands in favour of complimenting Kent upon his formal effects. Perhaps Kent's own lack of success in his chosen career of history painter derived from his lack of interest in its thematic aspects, whereas his delighted inventions for furniture or his drawings of landscape scenes declare his own basic predisposition for formal inventions. Kent's promotion as a landscape gardener took place at a time and in a circle of patrons and friends when learned themes were relished; but the very thrust of his own contributions, though he may have sought to please that circle of Palladians, ironically created a new taste which found little place for history painting and dramatic action in its preferred landscapes. To these declensions in garden history and their consequences for Kent's career we must now turn.

3 'Kentissime'

For Walpole, Kent's work at Esher was 'Kentissime'.[1] Such a claim implies both a progression in Kent's own development as a designer to this culmination and, what elsewhere in his *History of the Modern Taste in Gardening* Walpole clearly adumbrated, a Whiggish, progressive history of landscape gardening which Kent was largely instrumental in furthering. We must take up both these themes, looking first at what we can learn from a chronology of Kent's career, and then at his place in the annals of English garden history. Kent's gardens at Rousham, in Oxfordshire, are later than those at Esher; perhaps because of the accidents of survival they have more claim to constitute his *chef-d'oeuvre*, whatever Walpole claimed about Esher; so they will form an important link between those two topics.

Kent's career as landscape designer

A detailed chronology of Kent's landscape work is scarcely feasible, but the broad outlines are clear. So it should be possible to ask whether, given the cultural cross-roads at which the last chapter left Kent, he can be seen to have moved in any particular direction during the twenty-odd years during which he worked at garden designs. Was he opting more for gothick rather than classical, more for pictorial rather than poetic picturesque? Was he indeed following the road, which retrospectively Walpole mapped out for him, towards a

27 The obelisk in the ilex grove at Holkham (*photo: Geoffrey James*)

28 The Temple in the Woods at Holkham (*photo: Geoffrey James*)

complete naturalism? And if so, may we agree with Walpole over its significance?

Kent's specific landscape work begins as far as we know in the 1720s and early 1730s. He planned both a classical landscape at Holkham with Edward Coke, his travelling companion in Italy, and gothick commissions at Richmond for Queen Caroline. At Holkham the classical landscape involved an antique obelisk set in the groves of ilex, the classical 'oak',[2] as well as a triumphal arch, a neo-palladian temple and other Italian imagery (27 and 28; cat. nos 55 and 56). In Richmond Park the invocation of gothick was clearly a response to the Queen's determination to relate British intellectual history to her landscape park. Thereafter Kent seems to divide his favours fairly evenly between classical buildings like the Temple of Ancient Virtue at Stowe (8) and gothick ones like its Hermitage (see cat. no. 73). He worked for Pelham at Esher Place from 1733, and Kent's recently discovered designs for Esher show that he could envisage equally a classical and a gothick solution to that landscape with its surviving late mediaeval tower (cat. nos 81 and 113). At Chiswick, as befitted the villa of England's great Palladian architect, Kent's contributions were largely, but yet not wholly, classical. Rousham, dating from the very end of the 1730s, actually seems to preserve a deliberate and careful balance between the two forms. If anything, the classical emphasis predominates in the work of his final years at Holkham (though the broad outlines of a scheme may have been established there back in the 1720s), at Euston and at Badminton; but (as we shall see) the largeness of territory, which Kent could not wholly colonise with classical imagery, contributed in each of these cases a fundamental 'English' colour.

The gothick work for Queen Caroline has clear political and historical dimensions, making history pictures for Richmond Park. As Judith Colton has long since shown,[3] the contents of the Hermitage (busts of Newton, Locke, Boyle, Samuel Clarke and William Wollaston) were designed to 'Involve . . . the thoughts of [its] admiring guest'; or, as the same contemporary poetaster put it, 'The thinking sculpture helps to raise / Deep thoughts, the genii of the place'.[4] We must certainly see the programme as the Queen's, though its influence upon Kent's concept of architectural association may have been considerable; he was, after all, among the earliest in the eighteenth century to use three mediaeval subjects from the life of Henry V for British history paintings.[5] What the Queen wanted to proclaim were the British contributions of the new science to natural religion (and significantly an essay in the *Free Briton* of 16 August 1733 linked the Queen's national pride with her love of learning).[6] Yet it was not solely or simply a matter of the new British science. In addition to its effect on natural religion, the Scientific Revolution also had some connections with indigenous gothic architecture:[7] for empirical science, in setting itself against Cartesian system, had authorised the piecemeal exploration of the English countryside, not by some 'high priori road' but in the byeways where casual encounters with old buildings (later perhaps reported to the Society of Antiquaries) endorsed the notion that what was true was identical with what was localised.

How then should we judge the architectural style of the Richmond Hermitage? It seems to be a cunning mixture of classical with suggestions of native elements. In plan (see cat. no. 57) it was a Greek cross, and it was decorated inside in the classical taste: an altar, busts, and some Roman-looking sofas (29). Yet the outside gave the impression of being 'rudely laid together' (30); this structure was also termed 'grotesque', an ambiguous word

29 Interior of the Hermitage, Richmond Gardens, from J. Vardy, *Some Designs of Mr Inigo Jones and Mr William Kent*, 1744

30 Exterior of the Hermitage, Richmond Gardens, engraving, 1738

which for Kent especially implied antique ancestry,[8] as would the suggestion of an inscription over the main door and the triangular pediment. But the ruin effect of a missing pediment and only one turret (as Kent would also use for the Stowe hermitage), of appearing to sink it into the ground, and of the rough handling of the stonework which is echoed inside by the bands of rustication, all implied a more British ancestry, which the politico-philosophical message of course underlined. The pine trees briefly suggested in the Holkham drawing are nicely ambiguous, too: both northern and Italian. This double architectural suggestiveness parallels Caroline's invocation of sculpture by which, in Colton's words, she 'played the role of an ancient in modern times'. Her architect participated in this fine adjudication of a much vented rivalry, the so-called battle of ancients and moderns.[9]

For Merlin's Cave a few years later Kent insisted – as the name of the building authorised him to do – much more strongly upon an English style (31 and 32), with druidical roofs outside and natural materials (tree-trunks and branches) inside; he also designed for use there a silver standish with a gothick owl as the central lid finial.[10] Both the materials of the Cave and the sinking of the Hermitage into the ground clearly identify the British gothick with nature rather than with art, which was classical. Contemporaries

MERLINS CAVE

31 Exterior of Merlin's Cave, Richmond Gardens, engraving, 1730s

32 Interior of Merlin's Cave, Richmond Gardens, from J. Vardy, *Some Designs of Mr Inigo Jones and Mr William Kent*, 1744

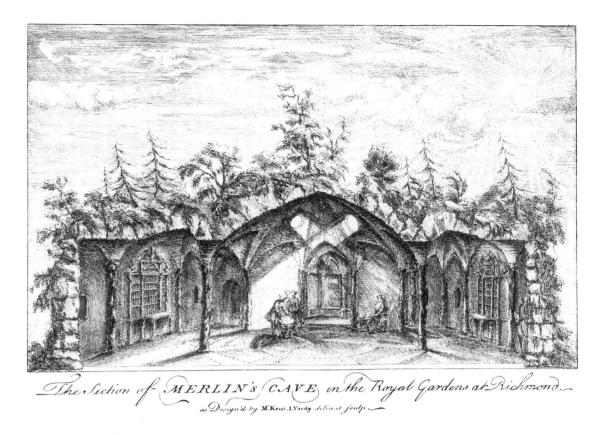

The Section of MERLIN'S CAVE *in the Royal Gardens at Richmond*
as Design'd by M.Kent.I.Vardy delin.et sculp

saw the Hermitage as a 'cave by nature made'. Its ruined turret announced, as do all ruins, the determining effects and contributions of nature and chance rather than art.

So right from what we take to be the start of his gardening career Kent was exploring (or was led by his patron to explore) not only the visual significance of gothick and antique architecture and decor but also the tensions between art and nature. And, further, if natural settings and materials signalled gothic culture or Englishness, then surely Kent's sensitive siting of classical buildings in landscape groves or other natural contexts must be interpreted as one way in which he continued to mediate or to compromise between the two available styles: it was his way of making Rome talk 'good English', perhaps with some slight, affected Italian accent. The early proposals at Holkham were for dominantly classical manipulations of the land (cat. nos 50 and 51); they gave way by the 1740s to far more skilful use of native scenery as surroundings for resonantly antique structures (cat. no. 53). Natural scenery was both indigenous and, properly treated, eloquent of the *boschetti* of Italian gardens and the groves of the Campagna, which we saw in chapter one were an important mediation between Italian and English gardens.

Other of Kent's early buildings spoke with these mixed tongues. The Temple of Venus set on the south-western bastion of the gardens at Stowe (33) derives its form from a mixture of Italian reminiscences: Woodbridge suggested Ligorio's courtyard for the Casino Pia in the Vatican or certain of Palladio's villas like Badoer,[11] but it is equally characteristic of Kent's delight in *capricci* that the Venus Temple would also allude to

33 The Temple of Venus, Stowe
(*photo: Stowe School*)

others like the Roman garden near Diocletian's Baths (34). But inside the temple was illustrated with scenes from Spenser's English epic-romance, *The Faerie Queene*. Spenser was what Kenelm Digby had called the 'English Virgil',[12] and if Kent was as sensitive as has been suggested to the theme of the progress of the arts he must have seen Spenser's major poem as a vital stage in poetic development from Virgil through Ariosto and Tasso (for whom Kent executed some illustrations)[13] to the eighteenth century.

The Temple of Venus suggests some effort, playful perhaps but still serious, to find an adequate decorum, of the sort Dryden had concerned himself with in painting, to achieve a due propriety in neo-classical garden designs for contemporary English estates. As early as 1715, in fact, Kent wrote to Massingberd from Italy of his determination to design a summerhouse 'agreeable to our climate';[14] perhaps we should not read that simply as a concern for practical exigencies but as an indication that Kent was already puzzling over the decorum required in such cases. In 1738 he would surely have seen and appreciated the significance of Batty Langley's substitution of a gothic termination point in a garden vista otherwise lifted wholesale from an engraving of the Villa Doria Pamphili.[15] As late as the 1750s Joseph Spence was still worrying about the propriety of antique sculptures and temples in English landscapes.[16]

After the early buildings for Richmond and Stowe Kent's most significant work was done, as Robinson reported in 1733, at Carlton House, Chiswick, Esher and Claremont. As we have already seen (above pp. 46–48), it is difficult to adjudicate Kent's work at the first: he was doubtless feeling his way, perhaps somewhat restrained on that particular site, and anxious to please Burlington who had probably proposed him for that task to the Prince of

34 Gardens and garden buildings facing the Baths of Diocletian, Rome, from Du Pérac's map of Rome, 1577

Wales. At Chiswick, other difficulties obtrude upon any clear definition of Kent's role in the gardens.[17]

Burlington had begun the gardens before his second Grand Tour and Kent's return from Italy in 1719. Another phase was inaugurated after Burlington's marriage in 1721, but it seems doubtful whether Kent was involved at this point, though, given his personality, it seems equally doubtful whether as the Burlington circle discussed, for example, the creation of the Tuscan temple fronting a sunken amphitheatre where an obelisk presides over a circular pool of water, Kent could have been kept out of such deliberations. The eclecticism of the contrivance seems rather Kentian, even if the classical emphases are Burlington's.

For the garden created at Chiswick was nothing if not deliberate: studied in both its classical tonality and in its adaptation of old and new Italy to the small English site. This last is important. Chiswick is a prime example of Palladio made to speak good English – the architectural equivalent to what Pope was doing for Homer in the 1720s.[18] Yet the scale reduces the classical models: either because they have to be accommodated to a small garden or because the very act of translation diminishes. John Macky noticed this in 1724 – 'Every walk terminates with some little building . . . another a little villa . . .'.[19] Even the villa itself translates sixty-eight Vincetine *piedi* of the Villa Rotunda into the smaller sixty-eight English feet. And this subtle attention to scale doubtless eliminated Kent's design for the exedra in the early 1730s (cat. no. 34) – it was used in the more spacious Elysian Fields at Stowe – while in its place a more modest semicircle of hedges and statues (cat. nos 35 and 36) replaced the grove which had originally reached up to the house.

More land to the west of the river had meanwhile been acquired in the late 1720s and this allowed for fresh developments in which Kent was clearly involved. These were the creation of an Italianate *boschetto* to the westward side of the river, a terrace (another Italianate feature, much needed on this flat site) on the south side flanking Burlington Lane, and the addition of the cascade. The large number of Kent sketches that survive for this last item suggests that he was involved, if only at the level of endless projections of

35 J. Rocque, engraved plan and views of Chiswick, 1736

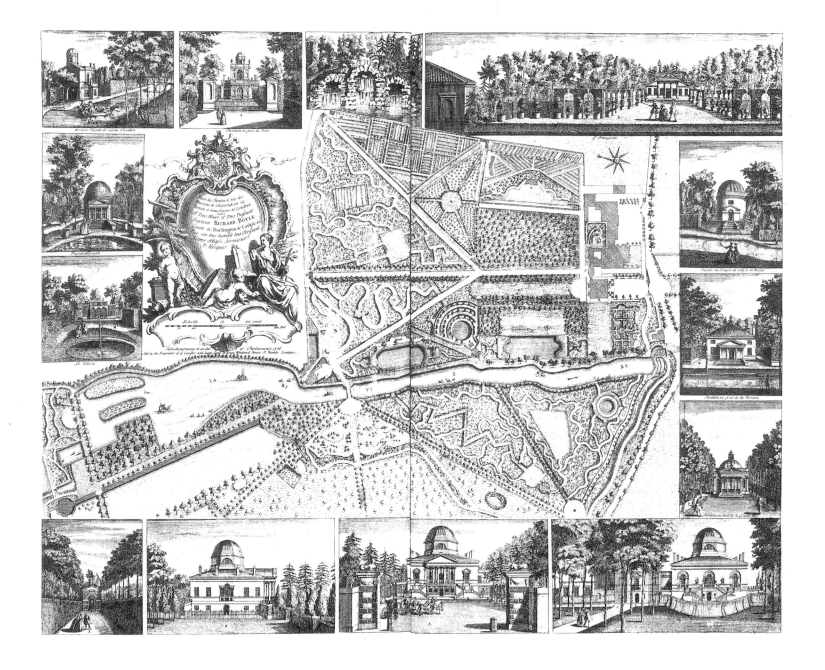

36 Engraved reconstruction of Pliny's villa at Tuscum, from Robert Castell, *The Villas of the Ancients Illustrated*, 1728

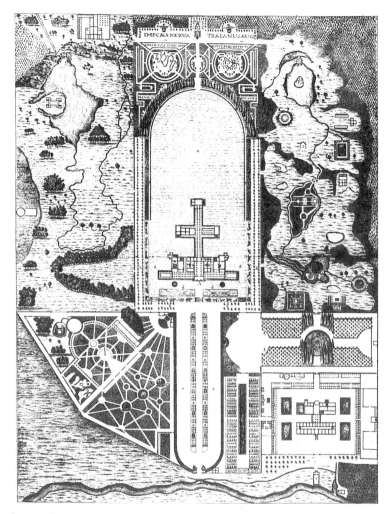

possibilities. Classical ones were canvassed (cat. no. 25); natural or gothick ones (cat. nos 26 and 29); even some compromises (cat. nos 28 and 97), though whether we would so read them without the survival of the other two kinds of design is doubtful. A classical head for the cascade would have sorted best with the wholly Italian air of the rest of Chiswick gardens. That a gothick and natural one was eventually chosen suggests either that the dialogue of styles, already discussed, was allowed its place in this privileged site of Palladian translation or (the more likely assessment) that it was seen to consort better with the natural effect of the *boschetto*, for which there were clear Italian prototypes (notably the decreasingly architectural fountains up the hillside at the Villa Aldobrandini, Frascati, as the controlled environment about the house surrendered to 'nature' further away). The treatment of this *boschetto* underlines its Italian accent: Rocque's plan of 1736 (35) shows serpentine walks opening into glades within the woodland, as at such Italian sites as the Villa Lante (see 14) and as Castell's *The Villas of the Ancients Illustrated* (36) proposed for the famous *imitatio ruris* of Pliny's villa.[20] But at Chiswick this woodland is crossed by three straight allées, which echo the same pattern in the main gardens and, more

37 J. Rigaud, drawing of the Obelisk near the south-west entrance to Chiswick, Trustees of the Chatsworth Settlement

importantly still, contrive a gardenist equivalent of Palladio's Teatro Olimpico. Rigaud's drawing of about 1733 (37) shows its effect – a very Kentian scene with spectators and actors, participants in a piece of garden history painting. The *coup de théâtre* is the obelisk with its funerary bas-relief from the Arundel marbles, originally given to the young Burlington in 1712; it establishes Burlington's gardens in the long progress of sculpture gardens that stretched from ancient Rome via Renaissance Italy to Jacobean and thence to Georgian England. It is here that Kent draws himself dreaming in the moonlight (cat. no. 27); here, too, that he planned a rustic temple before a flower garden (perhaps cat. no. 43).

Kent's involvement, then, at Chiswick is undeniable but still rather hazy as regards both dates and contributions. Spence dates his involvement from the late 1720s, which sorts with the initiation of the cascade and woodland; but he also elsewhere records that it was in October 1733 that 'Mr Kent was the sole beginner of the national, taste . . . at Chiswick'.[21] This discrepancy could simply mean that Spence knew Kent was involved in the gardens since the 1720s but registered a more 'natural' mode of design in the south-western parts in the 1730s. And Kent's work elsewhere in the 1730s – Stowe, Esher, Pope's Twickenham ('new works in his gardens yt I design'd there')[22] – would also have coloured that assessment of Kent's taste. Yet we must also recall that Kent's contribution to the main section of the gardens in the 1730s was the Italianate exedra, with its opening through a possibly Palladio-inspired screen of trees to the orangery garden (cat. no. 34), and perhaps the theatrical disposition of the Orangery (shown by Rocque in top right of 35) as well as the re-erection of the Inigo Jones gateway. Further evidence, too, of designs for garden ornaments that hardly constitute a natural taste continue during this period:[23] in 1738 Kent is providing 'Piedestalls for the Lions' and responding to Pope's request for vases (38).

Garden history, liking to insist upon England's steady progress towards naturalism, finds Chiswick difficult to assimilate. Kent's work at Claremont and Esher Place (especially now fresh drawings for the latter have come to light) may seem equally ambiguous, a mixture of softened geometry and calculated 'history paintings'.

At Claremont he worked, as he was to do at Rousham, over gardens laid out by other designers, in this case Bridgeman and Vanbrugh. The changes he inaugurated about 1729 are recorded in Rocque's plan of 1738 (39): they involve the breaking up of straight lines, levelling terraces (see cat. no. 60), removing walls and bastions, enlarging and serpenting the lake, and adding several garden buildings.[24] This last is a typical Kent taste for emphasising individual spots of a garden, focusing visitors' attention at specific points along their walk, and encouraging their participation in his ideas at locations where

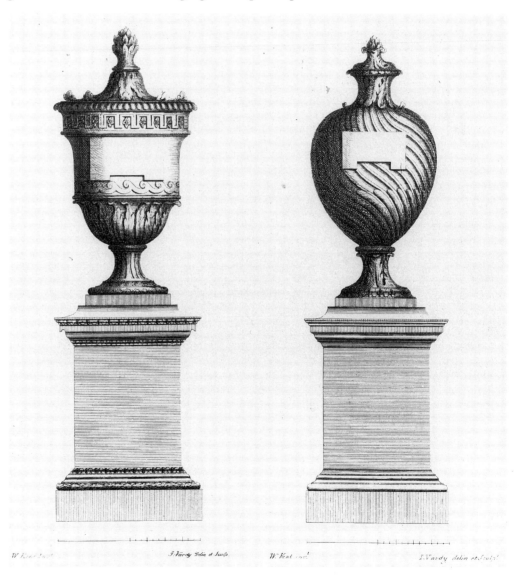

38 J. Vardy after William Kent, vases for Pope's garden, from *Some Designs of Mr Inigo Jones and Mr William Kent*, 1744

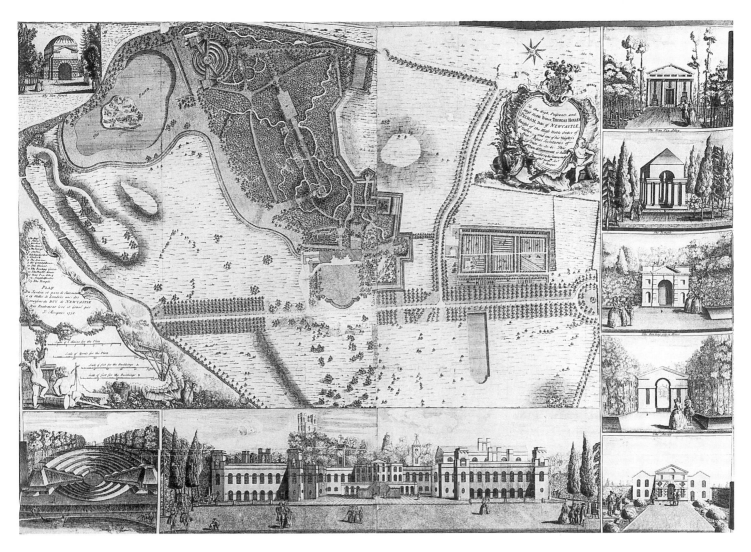

39 J. Rocque, engraved plan of Claremont, *circa* 1739 (*photo: Country Life Ltd*)

suggestions of stage or picture are clearly intimated by the design. His breaking of internal boundaries and letting one area flow into another encourages precisely that exploration which the garden buildings in their settings arrest at significant moments: exactly the account of Claremont which Whately gives later in the century (see above p. 46).

Tarrying and sauntering are perhaps endemic to the exploration of any garden, but Kent's drawings repeatedly emphasise precisely this activity. The alteration of the Claremont woodland between Vanbrugh's Belvedere and the bowling green involves more serpentine paths than Bridgeman had provided,[25] with more invitations to explore its groves, as a drawing in the Huntington Library suggests (40). Another drawing in the same collection and by the same artist (identified as George Lambert)[26] presents an emphatically georgic scene (41), which will become a central motif in Kent's landscapes during the rest of his career. In it, too, we see the curving edge of the woodland, the ha-ha which replaced the Bridgemanick bastions, and the new 'natural' lake with its cascade and temple. A

40 Attributed to George Lambert, the bowling green at Claremont, drawing, Henry E. Huntington Art Gallery, San Marino, California

41 Attributed to George Lambert, the new ha-ha and lake at Claremont, drawing, Henry E. Huntington Art Gallery, San Marino, California

42 J. Rocque, engraved view of the amphitheatre at Claremont, 1734

drawing in London (cat. no. 69) shows Kent exploring this particular scenery: but significantly he omits the ha-ha, allowing his scene a more pictorial or theatrical effect, the idea of which surely is exactly the Virgilian georgic scene that the other artist registered. He exaggerates the hillsides, makes the cascade head formally classical, and arranges his flocks, herds and pastoral characters so that two of the latter participate in the scene while two provide its audience. That such an emphatically theatrical scene is implied by Kent's sketch is endorsed by the proximity of Bridgeman's theatre which Kent retained and from which visitors would gaze down upon the lake (42). Nobody has ever remarked upon the significance of this striking feature. Kent would surely have recognised it, as Bridgeman's modern commentator did not,[27] as a grassy and hence Englished version of Bramante's exedra in the Vatican Belvedere, codified by Serlio and originally derived from the ruined Temple of Fortune at Praeneste.[28] At Claremont it is both stage and scenery, a platform from which to view Kent's naturalising of the land to represent Virgilian agriculture as well as an eloquent allusion itself to the progress of garden arts.

At nearby Esher Kent also did something to soften the severe geometric landscape he inherited (43). The groves to the south get serpentine walks, a favourite *boschetto* effect. Yet Rocque's plan of 1737 shows that Kent also retained some of the original geometry, including a triangular pond to the north; Esher thereby retains a mixed and varied aspect, surely reminiscent of the gardens and groves which Kent must have witnessed in Italy.[29] Equally the vignettes surrounding Rocque's plan testify to Kent's special design strategy

43 J. Rocque, engraved plan of Esher Place, 1737

of featuring individual buildings centred upon their own little 'stage'. The recently discovered drawings, however, suggest that Rocque's plan does not tell the whole story.

For one thing Kent evidently pondered a classical building, juxtaposed to the old mediaeval tower on the hillside below (cat. no. 81). The scheme that prevailed (cat. no. 82) incorporated that tower into the main house, leaving to the scattered buildings in the grounds the job of recalling classical ideas. It seems to have been a question of balance, of giving due weight to each historical style in the overall *ensemble* of Esher Place: this would explain the two versions of the Belvedere, which is not shown on Rocque's plan with the

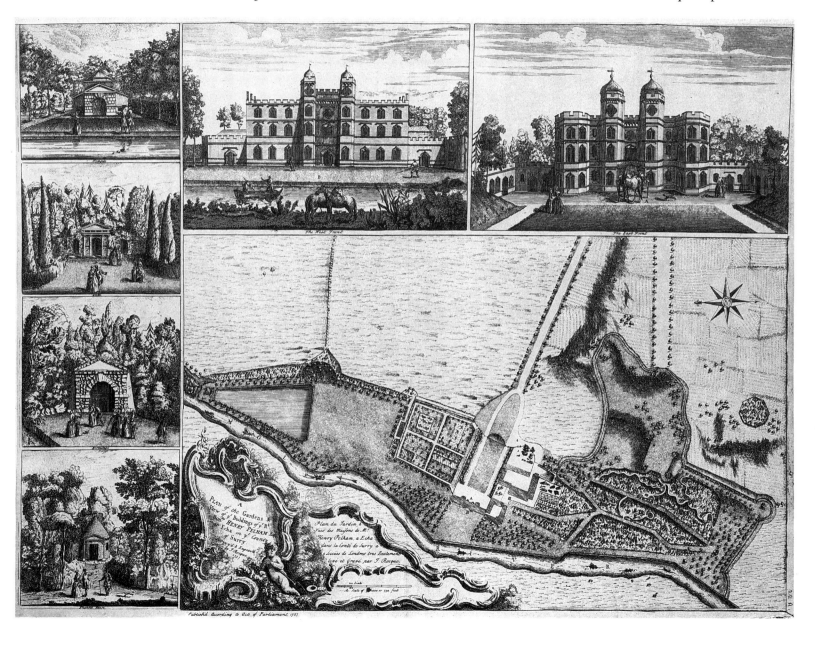

grotto, hermitage, temple and thatched house and may therefore be a later addition to the park – gothick in one drawing (cat. no. 68) where it balances the classical grotto, classical in another (cat. no. 111). Given that the latter is what was built, albeit without its turret, the sketch of the landscape may be construed as a first projection of the hillside.

The indigenous English landscape, according to the drawings, was required to play its part along with the old tower: Kent's sketches feature much skilful concern with opening and closing glades (cat. no. 87) and with careful screens admitting glimpses of classical buildings beyond (cat. nos 83 and 84), on which Thomas Whately commented.[30] The ground plan of what is arguably a flower garden (cat. no. 94) is especially intriguing: can it have been a proposal for the northern end (where Rocque shows the old triangular water fronted by a classical temple)? At any rate, it shows Kent by no means surrendering everything to 'natural' glades and grassy slopes, and it endorses the claims made for his introduction of flowers into gardens.[31] Then there are the various designs for tents and Chinese pavilions (cat. nos 89–93): if these were intended for Esher they suggest Kent's imaginative playfulness, an invention with fantastical designs that consorts well with his vision of the garden as theatre; indeed, these tents and pavilions could be projections for some festive event at Esher Place, an earlier version of the Watteau-like entertainment recorded here in 1763 by Horace Walpole.[32] It all suggests that maybe we have been too quick to interpret Pope's famous line upon Esher, 'Where Kent and Nature vye for Pelham's love'[33] as praise of his friend's natural bent. It could just as readily, and more aptly, signal that Pelham had to choose between Kent and Nature!

The rival claims of art and nature were much debated during this period of Kent's first major involvements in landscape work. The traditional *paragone* or contest between art and nature involved, too, the battles of the ancients and the moderns and of classical and gothic architecture, all of which lurk behind these gardens at Chiswick, Claremont and Esher. It is inconceivable that Kent was not an eager participant in discussions on these topics. His involvement in the 1720s with illustrations for John Gay's poetry certainly locates him right in the middle of such debates. His frontispiece for *Poems on Several Occasions* of 1729 and some of his designs for volume one of the *Fables* of 1727 seem to take up and in their own visual or architectural ways play with Gay's concerns.

Much of Gay's poetry attends to the sly and shifting boundaries between the arts of poetry or of society and their all too human, natural, subject matter. So in the frontispiece to *Poems* (44) Kent juxtaposes a classical temple, derived from Bramante's Tempietto in Rome,[34] to the tree: art versus nature. Classical putti appropriately are in the process of discovering an inscription, which a pastoral figure is also pointing out to his girl friend; but at the same time he seems to have his eye, not to mention his hand, upon more natural matters. A similar contrast of the achievements of art and the necessities of nature occurs, though more crudely, in the drawing (cat. no. 30) of the man and the dog both urinating in the grounds of Chiswick, its triumphal arch and classical obelisk both prominent. Kent's dogs, though less *in extremis* in other sketches, also frequently draw attention to un-bounded natural energies which the artificial garden and park cannot gainsay.

Gay's *Fables* take up the tug-of-war between art and nature, notably in 'The Painter who pleased Nobody and Everybody', in 'The Owls and the Sparrow', where the sparrow chides the Athenian birds for neglecting 'the ways by nature taught', in 'The Two

44 William Kent, engraved frontispiece
to Gay's *Poems*, 1720

Monkeys' and in 'The Jugglers', both of which address the topic of imitation and the limits
of verisimilitude: all of these Kent illustrated. Another, 'The Butterfly and the Snail', is a
parable of unchanging nature (the snail) and the upstart butterfly metamorphosed briefly
from an ugly worm. This last enquires loftily of the gardener whether his 'new arts correct
the year' and whether the garden exists only for such slimy scum as the snail. To this

45 Foudrinier after William Kent, illustration to Gay's 'The Butterfly and the Snail', 1727

debate Kent contributes his own witty gloss (45): a garden setting of exceptional artifice (a place very like those represented in drawings at Chatsworth wrongly ascribed to him)[35] – herms, a pergola, urns, a statue and a building that recalls the Casina at Chiswick. Yet it would be hard to conclude from this that Kent's preferences were for art at the expense of nature. Rather we should perhaps remark only – but it is supremely important – how alert he was to the boundaries, debates and even the compromises between art and nature. This is a theme to which his last few landscape designs were especially attentive.

If we look at the surviving drawings for Holkham, Euston and Badminton we see that Kent is required to work on extensive sites. His preference for a carefully contrived succession of spatial experiences, punctuated perhaps by 'set pieces' with their own surroundings, cannot be fitted into these expansive territories. What James Thomson called 'Claremont's *terrassed* height, and Esher's *groves*'[36] are not available in Norfolk or Suffolk or at Badminton in Gloucestershire. What he must do is site his own architectural contributions – triumphal arches at Holkham and Euston (cat. nos 55 and 48), the magnificent Worcester Lodge at Badminton (cat. no. 4) – in landscapes where, though he may adjust and shape a little, England's own resources have to serve his purpose. Nothing shows this more clearly than the two versions of the seat on the mount at Holkham.

The landscape at Holkham may have been planned in the 1720s before the house was built. The obelisk and the temple in the woods were established by 1729. During the 1730s Kent proposed a wholly Italianate setting for the seat on the rising ground to the south-west of the site for the house (cat. nos 50 and 51): there are herms at the entrance to the pergola tunnels, a metamorphic confusion of greenery and architecture, the theatrical space cleared like an arena with descending levels of a *cavea*, the seat itself centred and serving as both viewing platform and stage. It was an attempt to colonise a specific area within the much larger park with precise and detailed imagery. But a decade later this design was replaced by another (cat. no. 53): now the seat itself remains, classical enough, but it is absorbed, almost literally, into an indigenous countryside.[37] It is impossible to know exactly why the change was made. Perhaps Kent was indeed simply becoming more 'natural'; perhaps he had to realise that Holkham was too big a site to dominate with specific imagery and therefore to do so at one point would have been to maroon the seat too conspicuously on the mount in a sea of relatively untouched territory; perhaps, realising that, he made a virtue of necessity and achieved a forceful compromise – his extraordinary Palladian mansion and a few other classical items seen to be at home, Englished, naturalised, in the Norfolk countryside. Which explanation, if any, we choose for Holkham and the similar designs at Badminton and Euston may depend upon how we adjudicate Kent's surviving masterpiece.

Rousham

Horace Walpole considered that the gardens redesigned for General Dormer at Rousham in Oxfordshire were 'the most engaging of all Kent's works'; 'the whole is as elegant and antique as if the emperor Julian had selected the most pleasing solitude about Daphne to enjoy a philosophical retirement'.[38] On another occasion, after a further visit in the summer of 1760, Walpole told George Montagu that the 'garden is Daphne in little; the sweetest little groves, streams, glades, porticoes, cascades, and river imaginable; all the scenes are perfectly classic'.[39] As Walpole shrewdly registered, one of the most significant things about Rousham was the congruence of its classical or antique tone with its smallness, its miniaturisation. But that was not the whole story.

Kent was called to Rousham in the late 1730s and required to alter and extend the gardens which Charles Bridgeman had established there in the 1720s.[40] The site was oddly shaped, constricted on one side by the River Cherwell, on the west by the (then) boundary of Dormer property and towards the east by the old walled kitchen gardens and parish church. Bridgeman had very successfully colonised this garden area with square *basins*, shaped theatres and strong *allées* that held together the main segments of land (46). Kent had to accept the scale of the site as well as its unusual topography, but he developed and revised them to give the whole a truly Italianate colour and – perhaps even more important – significance as a garden history painting.

Kent was invited to Rousham by General Dormer in 1737, and he worked simultaneously on the house and gardens until 1741. The remodelling of the house will not be considered here, except to observe that Kent gave it the appearance of an older English building:

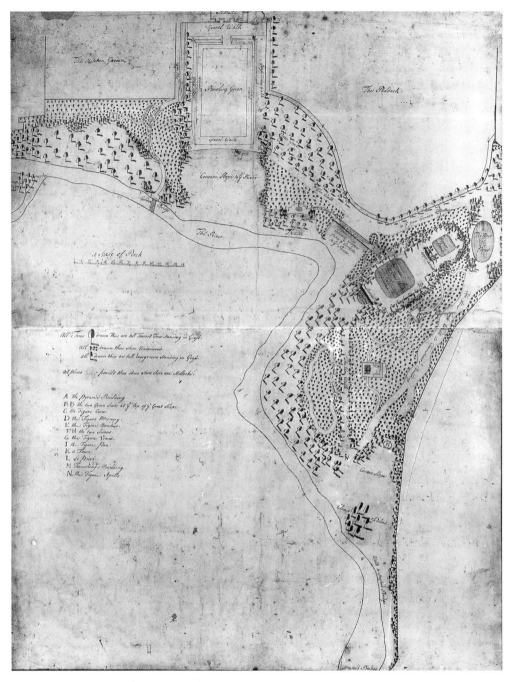

46 Estate plan of Rousham, sometimes attributed to William Kent or Charles Bridgeman, but likely to be by the steward, William White, *circa* 1738, Collection T. Cottrell-Dormer (*photo: Country Life Ltd*)

battlements, an ogee cupola and niches, mullioned windows (cat. no. 104). Inside these English effects were continued; but they were also matched with some classical mythological paintings on the ceiling of the parlour and some grotesque work in the antique manner. In all, the house declared a clearly English style yet in which are accommodated some strikingly Italian ingredients. And if visitors approached the gardens, not from the house but from the public road, they were treated to a similar conjunction – entering through a fine neo-classical gateway to be faced with a gothick seat and a view over fields towards the gothick house (47).

As this alternative approach to the gardens suggests, there is no required, programmatic route around Rousham, though the gardener John Macclary, who knew Kent, proposed one particular route from the house in a letter of 1750.[41] But as a recent modern survey shows, there are in fact over a thousand variations of the garden circuit 'none passing along the same walk twice and each leaving a significant level in the northern part of the garden unvisited, temptation for another day'.[42] The achievement of so much variety in such a small space is Kent's, capitalising on Bridgeman's, hallmark; further, such diversity ensured a perpetual alertness in the garden visitor, a readiness to respond to the 'scenes' as they were viewed, glimpsed or reached from different directions. Such receptivity was essential.

47 Classical gate and gothick seat, Rousham (*photo: Marianne Majerus*)

48 Scheemaker's Lion Attacking Horse, Rousham (*photo: Marianne Majerus*)

At the end of the bowling green in front of the house Kent placed Dormer's version of Scheemaker's copy of the sculpture of the *Lion Attacking the Horse* (48). This is one of many pieces which it was Kent's job to display, providing for them a garden setting in a direct line of descent from such English examples as Arundel's sculpture garden,[43] modern Roman ones that Kent would have seen for himself and classical ones read about in the literature of ancient Rome. But the lion and horse are not simply decorative. Even Macclary, concerned to recall for absent owners the physical experience of exploring their grounds, conveys the sense that the whole scene at the end of the bowling green has a meaning beyond its simply visual pleasures:

on each side is a fine large Green Tarrice Walk, at the end of which is two open groves, backt with two Naturial Hilloks planted with Scotch Firrs, and two Minervas upon Terms stands before them, and in the middle stands a Lion devouring a Horse, upon a very Large pedestal, you walk forward to view the Lion nearer, when your eye drops upon a very fine Concave Slope, at the Bottom of which runs the Beautifull River Charvell, and at the top stands two pretty Garden Seats, one on each side, backt with the two Hilloks of Scotch Firrs, here you sit down first in the one, and then in the other, from whence prehaps [sic] at this time you have the prettiest view in the whole World, Tho the most extensive part of it is but short, yet you see from hence five pretty Country Villages, and the Grant [sic] Triumphant Arch in Aston Field, together with the naturial turnings of the Hills, to let that charming River downe to butify our Gardens, and what stops our Long view is a very pretty Corn Mill, built in the Gothick manner but nothing sure can please the Eye like our Short View, their is a fine Meadow, cut off from the garden only by the River Charvell whereon is all sorts of Cattle feeding, which looks the same as if they was feeding in the Garden.

The 'prettiest view in the whole World'. Yet the sculpture of the lion and horse recalls one other, important vista elsewhere. From the platform beside the Fountain of Ancient Rome at the Villa D'Este in Tivoli, where another image of this lion and horse was placed (49), visitors to those magnificent gardens, having studied the model of ancient Rome, might turn and glimpse across the Campagna the outlines of the modern city. For Renaissance visitors there was perhaps the added point that this particular sculpture represented the old dominance of Tivoli (horse) by Rome (lion), a dominance now happily thrown off by the resurgence of the hilltown under the Este family.[44]

49 Fountain of Ancient Rome, Villa D'Este, Tivoli, from Falda, *Le Fontane di Roma* Pt IV (1675–1691)

But what is the visitor to make of this when he or she turns from the sculpture towards a smiling, English agricultural landscape at Rousham? At Tivoli we are asked to compare new and old, especially the new prestige which the Cardinal's gardens proclaim. Here at Rousham we also compare ancient and modern, classical and gothick, indigenous and foreign, as Macclary makes quite clear. In translating old Rome into modern England there are diminutions, even necessary absences, like those gaps which Alexander Pope left in the parallel texts of his *Imitations of Horace* to signal what could not be duplicated or what needed extrapolation from the Latin. At Rousham, antique and Renaissance Rome are there and not there, implied but eloquently absent.

It might be argued that this is too subtle, a nuance that is not 'there', even though Macclary seems to intuit such a meaning. But an even more explicit and eloquent statement a hundred yards away confirms that Kent did indeed want visitors' minds to respond in such a fashion. There had been terraces on the slope below the horse and lion as late as 1721, which Bridgeman presumably removed. But in the late 1730s Kent reintroduces this quintessentially Italian feature with his Praeneste Terrace, so called in a letter from Dormer's steward in 1740.[45] The Roman town of Praeneste (the modern Palestrina) boasted a famous Temple of Fortune; this classical ruin had been much studied by Renaissance architects and had inspired the design of one of the earliest of sculpture gardens, the Vatican Belvedere, and thence progressed through Europe to leave its mark, as we have seen, upon the grass theatre at Claremont.[46]

The Praeneste temple was much visited on the Grand Tour: Addison remarked upon 'fragments of this ancient temple' which 'stands high for the Advantage of the cool

Breezes, for which reason Virgil calls it *Altum* and Horace *Frigidum Praeneste*'.[47] Kent mimics that elevation at Rousham; the single arcade, with its urns, statues and benches (50), would have been a vantage point from which to absorb the English view. The 1738 estate map (see 46) also shows a path leading down to the arcade from the top of Praeneste, which is probably where a visitor would first arrive; this too parodies the means of descending the temple complex via steps at each end of its terraces. And just as the Roman temple could be excitingly seen from the Campagna[48] so Rousham's Praeneste is glimpsed down the Elm Walk once the visitor has circled the garden. However, Kent's terrace is but one row of arches; he has taken the famed succession of levels at Palestrina and reduced it to this elegant single line. Despite its name, it echoes many such loggias and arcades in Italian gardens (see 6 and 7) as well as the arcading of ancient baths studied in Burlington's *Fabbriche Antiche* of 1730. But its title calls attention to one precise model which has not been followed, perhaps which cannot be represented. Such are the difficulties of translating the classics into modern English.

Classical Rome enters the gardens in other ways, notably via the statuary.[49] Above the Praeneste Terrace a copy of the famous *Dying Gladiator* was originally to be placed upon an antique sarcophagus (cat. no. 42); at the end of the Elm Walk from which Praeneste is distantly viewed is a colossus (Apollo or Antinous). A copy of the Medici Venus presides over the little valley which takes her name. Yet northern and modern sculpture is also featured, notably figures by van Nost in the theatre, and these insist upon rival perspectives. Indeed, Venus, as the Roman goddess of gardens, is sited in a series of descending pools and cascades (51 and cat. no. 105) that draw distinctly upon modern Italian models: Kent's favourite rustic cascades at the Villa Aldobrandini and perhaps the various sequences of pools at the Medici villa of Pratolino where we know Kent was so excited by the gardens.

51 The Vale of Venus from the river, Rousham (*photo: Country Life Ltd*)

Kent's sketch of the Vale of Venus (cat. no. 105) shows the familiar actors/spectators engrossed in the drama of its history painting. What is the theme of the spectacle? If the distorted scale of the drawing is deliberate,[50] then the figures are dwarfed as they gaze in admiration at fountains at least five metres high, which would imply something about the scale of contemporary English imitations of classical and modern Italian gardens! Further, the statues representing a faun and Pan who lurk at its fringes, spying upon Venus, recall many Renaissance Ovidian pictures and stories. Kent's interest in Spenser may even have suggested to him, specifically, a version of the sixth book of *The Faerie Queene*, where Colin Clout and Sir Calidore are vouchsafed the vision of a Venus and the three graces.[51] A more elaborate iconography, based upon connections with the Elysian Fields at Stowe, has been proposed for the Venus Vale by David Coffin.[52] Yet it seems that while the garden is indeed learned, meaningful, in its commentary upon the progress of garden art and the accommodation of Italy in England, it is not offering an 'overall iconographical scheme'.[53] Rather it is the juxtapositions already noticed, ancient and modern, classical and gothick, natural and artificial, foreign and English, that constitute its 'subject'. This becomes more obvious once we address ourselves to the most conspicuous element at Rousham, the views beyond its garden.

It has already been mentioned that Kent 'extended' Bridgeman's garden. He did so in the sense that he forced our eyes outwards, as Macclary noticed, towards a rich agricultural landscape, to a 'Triumphant Arch in Aston Field' and to what was called the Temple of the Mill (cat. no. 106). Hal Moggridge has also more recently plotted the importance and variety of views outwards into the countryside.[54] This emphasis is especially featured at the theatre, where Kent softened the formal lines of Bridgeman's structure, retaining instead a semicircular glade backed by trees, on the edges of which grove are placed statues of Bacchus, Mercury and Ceres (52). Kent thereby must have actually transferred

52 The Theatre, Rousham
(*photo: Marianne Majerus*)

attention subtly from the theatre itself to its larger setting. This small pastoral clearing is both a stage upon which the statues (and visitors) 'perform' and a platform from which to view the land across the river. We may join those three statues and try to share their fabulous and mythic gaze. But we do not look entirely with their perspective.

The two items created by Kent outside the gardens are, to start with, aptly ambiguous. The eyecatcher, though rather gothick, was called a triumphal arch and is therefore Roman as well. The cottage-mill which is given a gothick frontispiece is also a temple dedicated to agricultural use. Both are rooted, almost literally, in the countryside of which Macclary was so proud. No visitor could help noticing it, partly because the wedge-shaped site draws in the views, partly because the open aspect of the gardens faces the meadows and rising hills to the north and north-west. The cattle across the river look 'as if they was feeding in the Garden'; in the paddock are 'fine Cows, two Black Sows, a Bore, and a Jack Ass'; beyond the kitchen gardens, is 'as pretty a set of pigg Stighs, as aney is in England'. Macclary notes, too, the prominence of Heyford Bridge – a view of which was deliberately incorporated into the gardens by altering the public road; he associates the bridge with 'commerce' ('Carriers Wagons') and with agriculture ('twenty Droves of Cattle goes by in a Day').

This rich and varied imagery of farming activity is manifestly English. But it is also equally Virgilian or georgic, if it is seen as the translation into practical English terms of a dominant theme of classical literature. Kent's friend, Pope, made exactly this point when he rendered Horace's georgic sufficiency on his Sabine Farm into humorous self-mockery:

> Content with little, I can piddle here
> On Broccoli and mutton, round the year;
> . . . .
> 'Tis true, no Turbots dignify my boards,
> But gudgeons, flounders, what my Thames affords.
> To Hounslow-heath I point, and Bansted-down,
> Thence comes your mutton, and these chicks my own:
> From yon old wallnut-tree a show'r shall fall;
> And grapes, long-lingring on my own only wall...[55]

Rousham, at least in Macclary's praise and doubtless in actuality as well, was more generously provided for by its surrounding agricultural land than Pope allowed of his. But the emphasis of the views from its garden was nevertheless of a landscape that more than adequately provided a modern and English equivalent of a traditional classical topos.

Rousham, then, recollects (quite literally) so much Italian-ness: antique Rome; the esteemed variety of modern Roman villas, gardens and groves; garden as theatre; garden as history painting. It even seems to work in part as a memory theatre of past culture, what Joseph Spence's eponymous character would use his garden for in *Polymetis* published in 1747, some few years after the Rousham gardens were finished and only one year after Kent's death.[56] But the antique, Italianate references and colour of Rousham are, like Polymetis's, accommodated in a purely English scene. The countryside, called into gardens as both Pope and before him the younger Pliny had advised,[57] places and defines the decorum of absorbing classical modes and forms into English life. Even inside the garden, all the specific allusions to classical and modern Rome are naturalised: temples designed for groves after the ancient manner[58] are ineluctably Englished when finally sited (cf. 53 and cat. no. 107).

Credit for such a vision of garden art need not be attributed solely to Kent himself. He moved easily and sympathetically in a circle of friends and patrons who were engaged precisely in assimilating Italy to England and in assessing how to be hospitable in Hanoverian England to the culture of classical Greece and Rome. All that we know about him – from his few letters, from the illustrations to Gay or the drawings at Chatsworth which may be projections for an illustrated *Dunciad* (his friend's domestication of the classical epic) – suggests a personality at once facetious, fantastic, quick-witted, and readily taken with the ideas and attitudes of his more learned companions.

Kent and English garden history

We have come now – inevitably – to the whole question of Kent's place in the development of the English landscape garden. Even Horace Walpole's proleptic and progressive historiography betrays an anxiety of influence. Though from the very start of his *History of the Modern Taste in Gardening* Walpole is determined to trace its happy outcome, this Whiggish perspective is nevertheless forced occasionally to address itself to questions of origins and influences. Thus, of Rousham he asks whether it was not 'probably on the model of Mr Pope's, at least in the opening and retiring shades of Venus's vale'.[59] That is entirely possible. Yet it has also been suggested above that this sense of progression through opening and closing scenes has other sources in Kent's career: his knowledge of Italian gardens where the same effects were constantly remarked upon, in print as early as 1624 in Wotton's *Elements of Architecture*;[60] his theatre work, especially his knowledge of Inigo Jones's masque designs which made a special feature of scene changing before one's eyes as if the stationary spectator were in fact moving through a metamorphic world. But such retrospective explanations have no place in Walpole's *History*. For him Kent appears 'bold and opinionative enough to dare and dictate, and born with a genius to strike out a great system from the twilight of imperfect essays'.[61] It was, Walpole explains, that 'more perfect perfection was still sought'; and 'improvements' (a word denoting both alterations to a garden *and* the amelioration of imperfect taste) were possible at a stroke under Kent's genius.[62] It is an excellent example of what Quentin Skinner has termed the 'mythology of prolepsis', whereby some event or action has to await the future to acquire meaning which is then read backwards into whatever needs historical explanation.[63]

We may begin to isolate what is not quite accurate about this version of garden history when Walpole comes to discuss Kent's management of water, perhaps (it is suggested) his greatest achievement. The passage matches its vision of 'improvement' with a suitably apocalyptic style:

> Adieu to canals, circular basons, and cascades tumbling down marble steps, that last
> absurd magnificence of Italian and French villas. The forced elevation of cataracts
> was no more . . .[64]

53 Townesend's Building, Rousham
(*photo: Marianne Majerus*)

But in Kent's drawing of the Vale of Venus at Rousham (cat. no. 105) we see two forced elevations of cataracts; and if the cascades do not tumble over marble, their clear descent (so to speak) from the rustic fountains of the hillside villa of Aldobrandini or from the pools at Pratolino by no means bids a final and decisive adieu to Italian gardens.

It is perhaps evident that Walpole's wish to see Kent as a 'more perfect perfection' than anything ever produced by any nation until that moment cannot really stand up to analysis. Walpole's self-confessed stance as 'the only unadulterated Whig left in England'[65] may explain his celebration of Kent's glorious revolution in garden design. The superlatives Walpole uses – 'Kentissime' or 'more perfect perfection' – alert us to his unabashed progressive emphases:

> We have discovered [in Kent's work at Esher] the point of perfection. We have
> given the true model of gardening to the world; let other countries mimic or corrupt
> our taste; but let it reign here on its verdant throne, original by its elegant
> simplicity, and proud of no other art than that of softening nature's harshnesses and
> copying her graceful touch . . . [66]

The rhetoric of what Richard Quaintance has wittily called 'Kent's messianic role [in] the harrowing of a horticultural hell'[67] is persuasive. Indeed, it has largely persuaded subsequent historians of the English landscape garden. But it is not the whole story, nor perhaps even the most interesting one. We have only to look at contemporary representations of Esher (54) to realise that other things have to be said. Kent's famous leap of the fence, too, is another dramatic flourish of Walpole's,[68] and we all remember it accordingly. But certainly Bridgeman utilised the ha-ha before Kent, and Kent's own experience of Italian gardens, whose variety almost always included views out into a rich countryside, would have made him at least aware of precedents.

54 Luke Sullivan, engraved view of Esher, 1759

. View of Esher in Surry the Seat of the late R.t Hon.ble HENRY PELHAM Esq.r .   Vue d'Esher dans la Comté de Surry Maison & Jardin magnifique du feu HENRY PELHAM Ecuyer. .

Published according to Act of Parliament : March 1.st 1759.   Printed for Rob.t Wilkinson in Cornhil, Carington Bowles in S.t Pauls Church Yard, Rob.t Sayer in Fleet Street, Hen.r Parker in Cornhil & John Boydell in Cheapside.

What is far more crucial than Walpole's concern with the uniqueness of Kent's achievement is the designer's own implicit recognition of and adjustment to changing ideas and tastes. His Italian experiences and, after his return from Italy, his position in the circles of Burlington and Pope, his dedication, albeit unsuccessful, to history painting, his participation in theatrical design – all these ensured that his garden designs would feature meaning and form in mutual cooperation, and that among his central concerns would be to teach Italianate and/or classicising effects to speak good English and to adapt themselves to English settings. Yet the 'Signior' was alert to new possibilities, quick and fertile in adjusting to new sites, new patrons, new demands in the perpetual contests between art and nature, between ancient and modern, between English and foreign.

Eight years after Kent's death, Isaac Ware, with whom Kent had been familiar, explained the new taste in gardening in his *Complete Body of Architecture:*

> What we propose now in gardens is to collect the beauties of nature; to separate them from those rude views in which her blemishes are seen, and to bring them nearer to the eye; to dispose them in the most pleasing order; and to create an universal harmony among them; that everything may be free, and nothing savage; that the eye may be regaled with the collected beauties of the vegetable world, brought together from the remotest regions, without that formality which was once understood to constitute the character of a garden; and that the further views be open to the horizons . . . . Our gardens are thus more regular than those of our ancestors, in effect more extensive; and throughout agreeable; everything pleasing is thrown open; everything disgustful is shut out; nor do we perceive all the art, while we enjoy its effects; the sunk wall prevents our knowing where the garden terminates: the very screen from unpleasing objects seems planted only for its natural beauty . . . [69]

Kenneth Woodbridge thinks that is a 'statement of [Kent's] aims' as a gardenist.[70] But it is surely only a part of them, the part that would prosper, leaving the more allusive, learned and Italianate elements to wither, neglected and unappreciated because new ideas had quickly overtaken them. Ware's emphasis upon the eye alone and his apparent sense of the nature that is to be imitated in gardens as solely vegetative are clear signs of those new perspectives.

It was amidst these new ideas, too, that Walpole wrote his *History* in the 1760s. By then Lancelot ('Capability') Brown's own distinctive style of landscaping was beginning to impose itself upon many English parks; and since Brown's style seemed (as *in part* it undoubtedly was) a large and radical application of Kent's 'natural' designs wholly in the spirit of Isaac Ware's analysis, Kent's own work was simply read in terms of its final apotheosis in Brown. We can perhaps register this later perspective in graphic fashion by comparing Kent's own sketches of Rousham with the painting by Thomas Jones of 1773 (55). The distance from his subject turns Rousham into a Brownian landscape in which natural forms, shapes and colours are the main ingredients, and the precise imagery of Venus, the cascades, and the various statues is absorbed into or hidden by the apparently 'natural' scenery.

Others, too, like Joseph Spence or Thomas Whately who praised Kent in terms similar to Walpole's, were also clearly influenced by developments under Brown. Spence, further-

more, had his own experience of designing gardens far less ambitious than Stowe or Rousham, and the suggestions he was in the habit of making for these much more modest estates rarely included the classical statues and temples that would have contributed their essential colours and themes to garden history paintings. Spence, indeed, offers useful information by which to explain how the estimates of Kent's work which he himself, Whately and Walpole made were culturally determined.

Spence's *Polymetis*, published the year before Kent died, was an enquiry into the old sisterhood of the arts, *ut pictura poesis*. But Spence undertakes the enquiry precisely because he claims that the meanings of classical imagery are no longer understood. His eponymous character singles out the garden statuary at Versailles, 'the collections in Rome itself' as well as Cesare Ripa's book of emblems as examples of a classical visual language now partly lost – 'we are frequently at a loss to know what they mean'; nor can he understand that part of Rubens's Whitehall ceiling where 'cupids . . . conduct a triumphant sort of car, drawn by wild lions'.[71] But as D. J. Gordon showed in a magnificent essay on 'Ripa's Fate' this inability was caused by Polymetis's ignorance of one of Alciati's emblems which represented the power of love as a cupid taming the wildest of beasts by driving them in a chariot.[72] This loss of intimacy with classical languages and their Renaissance systemisation is why Spence's character sets out to collect all verbal and visual references to classical deities and to display them in a series of temples scattered round a landscape garden 'rather wild than regular'. It is quite literally a classical memory theatre set in an English landscape park. What is above all crucial for our purposes about *Polymetis* is that its author enjoyed his considerable classical learning, especially its verbal/visual configurations, at the same time as he realised that it was fast becoming a lost language. This double response doubtless explains the book's popularity in the years after Kent's death: there were further editions in 1755 and 1774 as well as a school version of 1764 which went into six editions.

Now *Polymetis* is representative of an important shift in taste and learning which would have consequences for both the interpretation of Kent's landscape work and for that work itself. These changes also include that movement in theories of painting from poetic to pictorial composition which was discussed above (pp. 33 ff.). They involved a whole series of realignments whereby learned subject matter and above all the primacy of human action in art surrendered to a concern for execution, formal interests, the pleasures of shape, line and colour. Kent himself reveals that he shared in some of these realignments, while Walpole's judgements on him typify the final triumph of pictorial or picturesque composition which had, in the first flush of its success, chosen to misread the essentially interim nature of Kent's achievements. It is worth sketching briefly some of the reasons for these changes which so affected Kent's gardenist work and estimates of it; five factors may be isolated, though it should be stressed that they are given here with far more coherence and sense of pattern than they in practice enjoyed.

There was, first, a shift in the patronage of artists and gardenists from the aristocracy and upper classes, for whom the Grand Tour, the heritage of Rome and its attendant verbal/visual languages were axiomatic, to far less learned gentry and bourgeoisie; or, if still equally learned as many of the new patrons were, far less concerned to parade that learning or make it a central concern in their landscapes. Second, this new patronage looked rather to Dutch art for its collections than to the classical modes and subjects of Nicolas Poussin or Claude Lorrain – and Dutch art was not primarily associated with the traditions of *ut pictura poesis*.[73] Third, the territory of the British Isles, like the Dutch countryside, was explored and looked to for its own subject matter: the language of classical let alone neo-classical imagery was not endemic to Britain. Indeed, as early as the time of Inigo Jones, his friend Edmund Bolton declared of Stonehenge that 'The dumbness of it... speakes; that it was not any worke of the ROMANS. For they were wont to make stones vocall by inscriptions...'.[74] Fourth, travel increasingly familiarised men with the great mountainous areas of Europe – the Alps, Snowdonia, the English Lakes or even the Derbyshire Peak, the Scottish Highlands: not only did these seem far less susceptible of translation into classical verbal and visual languages, but Edmund Burke largely defined the sublimity of such regions in terms of the inexpressible.[75] Travel, too, subtly and slowly undermined one of the key concepts of traditional aesthetics: the imitation of nature for Dryden had meant human nature; increasingly now it meant nature. Fifthly and finally, the theatre of action in a garden involved the mind of the spectator himself. Locke's epistemology and its development by his English eighteenth-century successors gave to the individual mind an enormous power, power to shape itself – even if the shaping was sometimes fairly mechanical – in unique ways. How one mind interpreted and used images which its sight provided was potentially quite unlike any other mind; certainly, there were conservative rearguard actions fought to preserve a universal and general map of human experience, but paths were opened to the authority of the individual sensibility.[76]

The effect of these movements of ideas, taste and patronage upon gardens has often been noted: just as the learned Spence was sceptical of the efficiency of classical languages, so others with similar classical skills found themselves dissatisfied with learned and artificial gardens. Joseph Warton wrote:

> Lead me from gardens deck'd with art's vain pomps.
> Can gilt alcoves, can marble mimic gods,
> Parterres embroider'd, obelisks, and urns
> Of high relief; can the long spreading lake,
> Or vista lessening to the sight, can Stow,
> With all her attic fanes, such raptures raise
> As the thrush haunted copse....[77]

This reaction was set out more systematically by Thomas Whately some twenty or so years later, when, distinguishing between emblematic and expressive gardens, he opted for the latter because they yield 'transitory' images that are 'not sought for, not laboured, and have the force of a metaphor, free from the detail of allegory'. Whately, in fact, argues energetically that what serves well in paintings need not or will not be apt in gardens.

In this emphasis on what Spence called 'the clearest language of things themselves'[78] can be glimpsed the genesis of that picturesque fad which swept England by the end of the eighteenth century, sustained by the writings of William Gilpin, Richard Payne Knight and Uvedale Price. Some of these latter-day picturesque commentators sought to absorb Kent, seeing him as an inspired precursor of their successful concerns. But Price declined to see Kent as picturesque, and that seems a sounder historical judgement. Kent may have worked for Whigs, but that is no good reason for writing him into a Whiggish garden history. Instead we should seize the chance of using Kent's peculiar position to chart the developments in garden design at an obviously crucial moment.

Kent has proved difficult to 'place'. It is easy enough to see how his designs were susceptible to claims for their naturalness. For example, his work for Henry Furnese at Gunnersbury Park,[79] which can be deduced from comparing two maps of 1741 and 1777 (56), involved the elimination of tight little geometric compartments and throwing the estate into a parkland where odd incidents – ponds, maybe small buildings or statues – are screened by trees, yet glimpsed and inviting. It all seems to announce the Brownian style of the years after Kent's death. But if we also register that Kent's changes at Gunnersbury provided an apt setting for John Webb's mansion, an adaptation of Palladio's Villa Badoer, we can also see how he has achieved an entirely suitable English version of classical and Italian *imitatio ruris*. Essentially the same translation was what Kent was providing at Holkham, Euston, Badminton – all, like Gunnersbury, places where he worked in the 1740s.

Gunnersbury suggests what designs for Holkham confirm, that Kent was moving, for whatever reasons, towards the 'natural'. We have already seen (above, p.79) how between the mid 1730s and the mid 1740s he altered the design for the seat on the mount. This suggests that an earlier ambition to establish elaborate scenery within sight of the mansion was abandoned in favour of using architectural features to mark the highpoints of these large sites. The obelisk, the temple in the woods, the twinned pavilions and arch-lodge at Holkham were all probably established or planned in the 1730s, and in the following decade the mount seat was also established on the crown of a natural-looking hillside. At Euston a similar and more successful attempt was made to realise the natural potential of the land as an ideal setting for the neo-Palladian mansion echoed in two directions by a temple-like pavilion and a triumphal arch (cat. nos 48 and 49).

Euston and Holkham, like Badminton to which we shall turn shortly, were all large estates; it would have been scarcely possible, even if Kent had wanted, to colonise such an extent of ground with statues and buildings as at Stowe or Rousham. Such a density of meaningful items was anyway, as we have seen, less popular, whether on account of the expense or for more complicated intellectual factors. In 1751, for instance, Walpole went out of his way to say that he liked Stowe's 'Albano glut of buildings, let them be ever so much condemned'.[80] Kent's last commissions eschew any glut of buildings, but they do continue to delight in essential touches of classicising imagery set at key points in the English countryside. Kent was presumably quite capable of gothicising images. But at Euston, Holkham and Badminton the eye seeks out and marks the antique air of arches and temples, the Roman tincture they lend to English green.[81] Alternatively, once reached, these buildings offer refuge within the safety of a privileged past style to view the parkland, *tout pur*. But pure is precisely the word, for Kent's care in either ordering the natural face of the countryside or carefully controlling what parts of it may be seen is in the interests of *la belle nature*, nature brought to her perfection by art.[82] Not for nothing had Kent participated in John Gay's various publications, where the claims and rivalries of art and nature were such a central theme. Twenty years or so later such questions were still alive; indeed, the changes and declensions in the midst of which Kent needs to be seen were marked by a constant attention to the exact ratio of art and nature. Kent's infamous clumps are a case in point (cat. no. 54): Walpole ridiculed them – 'the lawn looks like a ten of spades'[83] – and he was right. But their failure draws attention to how Kent was trying to get right the balance of art and nature as well as the scale on which that had to be done. Walpole's remark

56 Gunnersbury Park, West London, two maps of 1741 and 1777 (*photo: Country Life Ltd*)

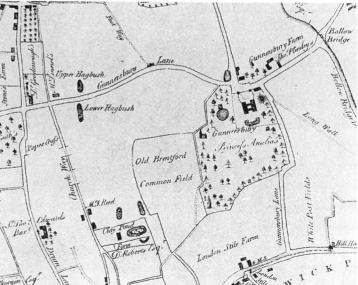

continues – 'Clumps have their beauty; but in a great extent of country, how trifling to scatter arbours, where you should spread forests'.

Kent's *forte* had been, so to speak, arbours not spreading forests. Many of his designs offer some specific building in its own suggestive setting; these natural settings were used to enhance the artificial elements at their centre, often indeed to create a clearing or amphitheatre for the 'event' of which the building formed both subject and backdrop. Such incidents, arranged around a larger but not too extensive landscape, gave interest to or enlivened the scene. Lord Lovell, later Earl of Leicester and Kent's patron at Holkham, knew exactly how his protégé despised 'damned dull walks... these unpictoresk those cold & insipid strait walks wch make the signior sick, to think that they, wch even Mr Pope himself cd not by description enliven...'.[84] The emphasis is revealing: Kent wants scenes which, like pictures, have interest (even human interest) and bear description (i.e. have some subject matter to be described). Kent's earliest work was to give animated focus to some part of a larger landscape: thus he had in 1734 provided Kensington Gardens with the Queen's Temple at an angle in two walks and gave its visitors a view of the Serpentine.[85] And in the 1740s he almost certainly provided a Palladian, octagonal summerhouse for Philip Southcote at Woburn Farm.[86] And this was still his instinct in the really larger estates like Badminton. There remain designs for some artificial elements near the house (cat. nos 1–5), but the Canaletto painting (57) of about 1748, the year of Kent's death, must indicate quite accurately what he had done. The eye is led relentlessly across country – an

57 Canaletto, *Northward view in the park at Badminton*, painting of late 1740s, His Grace the Duke of Beaufort

58 Worcester Lodge, Badminton
(*photo: Jeremy Whitaker*)

apt, horseman's invitation. But three miles away on the horizon Kent placed one of his most magnificent buildings, Worcester Lodge: brilliantly eclectic, suggestive of Palladian wings, Serlian gateways; from inside, beneath the ceiling mouldings of the Seasons, it is an ideal temple from which to view the changing year in this Gloucestershire countryside.[87] Its theatrical panache is wholly Kentian: itself a stage setting, Worcester Lodge is also a termination point for various cuts through the surrounding woodland (58).

There is much at Badminton, as at Euston and Holkham, which marks the double focus of English garden design in the mid 1740s. On the one hand, the sweep of Brownian parkland *avant la lettre*: 'the beauties of the place, as wood, water, hill and vale, the concave and convex of Mr Kent', or again, 'the trees, lawns, concaves, all in the perfection in which the ghost of Kent would joy to see them'.[88] On the other hand, the construction of garden history paintings or dramas focused around some classical or gothic building where its visitors are both spectators and participants in the action. If the one aspect of Kent's work prospered in Brown, then the other attention to specific, autonomous buildings in their own apt settings flourished in Thomas Wright, who worked at Badminton after Kent, and in Thomas Robins, as well as having an influence far beyond the British Isles.[89] Garden

59 The caryatids from Kent's seat on the mount at Holkham, now at Burnham Overy Town (*photo: Geoffrey James*)

historians remember the Brownian legacy of Kent, no doubt because it prospered so extravagantly; but they forget and often neglect to cherish the other which drew its strengths from cultural concerns now less fashionable and certainly less understood.

Richard Hurd seemed to identify this problem of historical understanding in 1762. Writing about Edmund Spenser, whom Kent had clearly enjoyed, Hurd pauses in his comparison between the focus of action in a classical epic and the series of related actions in *The Faerie Queene* to draw an analogy with garden design. It will serve as a final comment, typical of a need to annex Kent's designs to a taste which came to its climax only after his death, yet more than usually sympathetic to alternative perspectives even if it cannot, as this assessment of his landscape designs has tried to do, locate Kent within them:

> This Gothic method of design in poetry [i.e. Spenser's] may be, in some sort, illustrated by what is called the Gothic method of design in gardening. A wood or grove cut out into many separate avenues or glades was amongst the most favourite of the works of art which our fathers attempted in this species of cultivation. These walks were distinct from each other, had, each, their several destination, and terminated on their own proper objects. Yet the whole was brought together and considered under one view by the relation which these various openings had, not to each other, but to their common and concurrent centre. You and I are, perhaps, agreed that this sort of gardening is not of so true a taste as that which Kent and Nature have brought us acquainted with, where the supreme art of the designer consists in disposing his ground and objects into an *entire landscape* and grouping them, if I may use the term, in so easy a manner that the careless observer, though he be taken with the symmetry of the whole, discovers no art in the combination... This, I say, may be the truest taste in gardening, because the simplest. Yet there is a manifest regard to unity in the other method, which has had its admirers – as it may have again – and is certainly not without its *design* and beauty.[90]

Bibliography and list of abbreviations

The following is a bibliography of writings on or relevant to William Kent,
listed alphabetically by abbreviations used throughout the notes and catalogue.

APOLLO OF THE ARTS *Apollo of the Arts: Lord Burlington and his Circle*, catalogue of exhibition at University of Nottingham, 1973

BATEY Mavis Batey, 'The way to view Rousham by Kent's gardener', *Garden History*, 11/2 (1983), pp.125–32

BLUNT *Treasures from Chatsworth*, ed. A. Blunt (London, 1979)

BOUTWOOD James Boutwood, 'Poet's Essay in the Picturesque: Alexander Pope's Garden at Twickenham', *Country Life*, CXLIII (7 March 68), pp.512–14

BURLINGTON Richard Boyle, Earl of Burlington, *Fabbriche Antiche Disegnate da Andrea Palladio* (London, 1730)

BRADLEY Laurel Bradley, 'Eighteenth-century paintings & illustrations of Spenser's *Faerie Queene*: a study in taste', *Marsyas*, 20 (1979–80), pp.31–51

BROWNELL Morris Brownell, *Alexander Pope and the Arts of Georgian England* (Oxford, 1978)

VON BUTTLAR Adrian von Buttlar, *Der englische Landsitz 1715–1760. Symbol eines liberalen Weltentwurfs* (Mittenwald, 1982)

CARRE 1973 Jacques Carré, 'Lord Burlington's Garden at Chiswick', *Garden History*, I/3 (1973), pp.23–30

CARRE 1977 Jacques Carré, 'Architecture et paysage: le jardin de Chiswick', *Jardins et Paysages: le Style Anglais*, ed. André Parreaux and M. Plaisant, 2 vols. (Lille, 1977)

CARRE 1980 Jacques Carré, *Lord Burlington (1694–1753). Le connaisseur, le mécène, l'architecte*, doctoral thesis presented to the University of Dijon, 1980, 3 vols.

CARRE 1982 Jacques Carré, 'Through French Eyes: Rigaud's Drawings of Chiswick', *Journal of Garden History*, II (1982), pp.133–42

CASTELL Robert Castell, *The Villas of the Ancients Illustrated* (London, 1728)

CHATSWORTH Materials from the Devonshire Collection held at Chatsworth (Trustees of the Chatsworth Settlement)

CLARK H. F. Clark, 'Lord Burlington's Bijou, or Sharawaggi at Chiswick', *Architectural Review*, 74 (1944), pp.125–9

CLARKE 1973 George B. Clarke, 'Grecian Taste and Gothic Virtue: Lord Cobham's Gardening Programme and its Iconography', *Apollo*, 97 (1973), pp.566–71

CLARKE 1974 George B. Clarke, 'William Kent: Heresy in Stowe's Elysium', *Furor Hortensis: essays on the history of the English landscape garden in memory of H. F. Clark*, ed. Peter Willis (Edinburgh, 1974), pp.48–56

COFFIN David R. Coffin, 'The Elysian Fields of Rousham', *Proceedings of the American Philosophical Society*, 130 (1986), pp.406–23

COLTON 1974 Judith Colton, 'Kent's Hermitage for Queen Caroline at Richmond', *Architectura*, IV (1974), pp.181–91

COLTON 1976/7 Judith Colton, 'Merlin's Cave and Queen Caroline: Garden Art as Political Propaganda', *Eighteenth-Century Studies*, 10 (1976–7), pp.1–20

COLVIN 1968 Howard Colvin, 'Georgian architects at Badminton', *Country Life*, CXLIII, (4 April 1968), pp.800–804

COLVIN Howard Colvin, *A Biographical Dictionary of British Architects 1600–1840* (1978)

COX Trenchard Cox, 'William Kent as a Painter', *Artwork*, 7 (1931), pp.28–36

CROFT-MURRAY E. Croft-Murray, 'William Kent in Rome', *English Miscellany*, I (1950), pp.221–9

DAVIS Terence Davis, *The Gothick Taste* (Newton Abbot, 1974)

EICHHOLZ Jeffrey P. Eichholz, 'William Kent's Career as Literary Illustrator', *Bulletin of the New York Public Library*, 70 (1966), pp.620–46

FLEMING John Fleming, 'William Kent at Rousham; an eighteenth-century Elysium', *Connoisseur*, CLIII (1963), pp.158–65

HARRIS 1959 John Harris, 'A William Kent Discovery', *Country Life*, 125 (14 May 1959), pp.1076–8

HARRIS 1983 John Harris, 'William Kent's Gothick', *A Gothick Symposium* (London: The Georgian Group, 1983)

HARRIS 1986 John Harris, 'William Kent's drawings at Yale and some imperfect ideas upon the subject of his drawing style', *Essays in Honor of Paul Mellon*, ed. John Wilmerding (Washington, D.C., 1986), pp.136–53

HARRIS 1987 John Harris, 'Esher Place, Surrey', *Country Life*, CLXXXI (2 April 1987), pp.94–7

HASSALL I W. O. Hassall, 'Ilexes at Holkham', *Garden History*, VI/1 (1978), pp.58–60

HASSALL II W. O. Hassall, 'Clumps', *Garden History*, VI/2 (1978), pp.22–5

HECKSCHER Morrison Heckscher, 'Eighteenth-century rustic furniture designs', *Furniture History*, 11 (1975), pp.59–65

HODSON Peter Hodson (compiler), *William Kent: a Bibliography and Chronology* (Charlottesville, Va., 1964)

HONOUR Hugh Honour, 'John Talman and William Kent in Italy', *Connoisseur*, 134 (1954), pp.3–7

HOUSE IN TOWN David Watkin, Antony Ratcliff, Nicholas Thompson and John Mills, *A House in Town*, ed. Peter Campbell (London, 1984)

HULL *A Tercentenary Tribute to William Kent*, catalogue by Harold Barkley, Geoffrey Beard, Madeline Edmead, Terry Friedman, Cinzia Sicca and John Wilton-Ely (Kingston Upon Hull, 1985)

HUNT 1976 John Dixon Hunt, *The Figure in the Landscape. Poetry, Painting and Gardening during the 18th century* (Baltimore, Md., 1976)

HUNT 1983 John Dixon Hunt, 'Pope's Twickenham Revisited', *Eighteenth-Century Life*, VIII n.s.2 (1983), pp.26–35

HUNT 1985 (I) John Dixon Hunt, 'Ut pictura poesis, ut pictura hortus, and the picturesque', *Word & Image. A Journal of Verbal/Visual Enquiry*, I/1 (1985), pp.87–107

HUNT 1985 (II) John Dixon Hunt, 'William Kent and the Theatre', *Kunstlicht* (Vrije Universiteit, Amsterdam), 16 (1985), pp.9–12

HUNT 1986 John Dixon Hunt, *Garden and Grove. The Italian Renaissance Garden in the English Imagination 1600–1750* (London, 1986)

HUNT 1987 John Dixon Hunt, 'William Kent's work as illustrator', *Illustrations in English Literature*, ed. Joachim Möller (forthcoming 1987)

HUNT AND WILLIS *The Genius of the Place. The English Landscape Garden 1620–1820*, ed. John Dixon Hunt and Peter Willis (London, 1975)

HUSSEY, 'ROUSHAM' Christopher Hussey, 'A Georgian Arcady – William Kent's gardens at Rousham, Oxfordshire', *Country Life*, XCI (14 and 21 June 1946), pp.1084–5

HUSSEY Christopher Hussey *English Gardens and Landscapes 1700–1750* (London, 1967)

JACQUES 1976 David Jacques, 'The Art and Sense of the Scriblerus Club in England, 1715–35', *Garden History*, IV (1976), pp.30–53

JACQUES 1983 David Jacques, *Georgian Gardens. The Reign of Nature* (London, 1983)

JOHNSON I Francis Johnson, 'The Bicentenary of William Kent', *Transactions of the Georgian Society for East Yorkshire*, II/ii (1948), p.24

JOHNSON II Francis Johnson, 'William Kent and Bridlington', *Country Life*, 104 (9 July 48), p.88

JONES, DESIGNS *The Designs of Inigo Jones*, 2 vols. (London, 1727)

JOURDAIN Margaret Jourdain, *The Work of William Kent – Artist, Painter, Designer and Landscape Gardener* (London, 1948)

KENT William Kent, *The Designs of Inigo Jones, Consisting of Plans and Elevations for Publick and Private Buildings*, 2 vols. (London, 1727)

KENT JOURNAL William Kent's Italian journal, 1714, The Bodleian Library MS Rawl. D. 1162

KENT LETTERS BODLEY Bodleian Library MS Eng. Misc., c114

KENT LETTERS LINCOLN William Kent's letters from Italy to Burrell Massingberd, Lincolnshire Archives, Lincoln

LEATHERBARROW David Leatherbarrow, 'Architecture and situation: a study of the architectural writings of Robert Morris', *Journal of the Society of Architectural Historians*, XLIV (1985), pp.48–59

LEES-MILNE J. Lees-Milne, *Earls of Creation; Five Great Patrons of Eighteenth-Century Art* (London, 1962)

MACK 1969 Maynard Mack, *The Garden and the City. Retirement and Politics in the Later Poetry of Pope* (Toronto, Buffalo and London, 1969)

MACK 1985 Maynard Mack, *Alexander Pope. A Life* (New Haven, Connect., 1985)

MARTIN Peter Martin, *'Pursuing Innocent Pleasures'. The Gardening World of Alexander Pope* (Hamden, Connect., 1984)

MIDDELDORF Ulrich Middeldorf, 'William Kent's Roman Prize in 1713', *Burlington Magazine*, XCIX (1957), p.125

MOGGRIDGE Hal Moggridge, 'Notes on Kent's garden at Rousham', *Journal of Garden History*, VI (1986), pp.187–226

NEAVE David Neave, 'Lord Burlington's park and garden at Londesborough, Yorkshire', *Garden History*, VIII (1980), pp.69–90

NOKES David Nokes, 'Pope's epigrams on William Kent: a new manuscript', *Yearbook of English Studies*, 5 (1975), pp.109–14

POPE, CORRESPONDENCE *The Correspondence of Alexander Pope*, ed. George Sherburn, 5 vols. (Oxford, 1956)

POPE, POEMS *The Twickenham Edition of the Poems of Alexander Pope*, ed. John Butt, 10 vols. (London, 1938–67)

PUGH Simon Pugh, 'Nature as a Garden. A conceptual tour of Rousham', *Studio International*, CLXXXVI (October 1973), pp.121–25

QUAINTANCE Richard E. Quaintance, 'Walpole's Whig Version of Landscaping History', *Studies in Eighteenth-Century Culture*, 9 (1979), pp.285–300

ROCOCO *Rococo. Art and Design in Hogarth's England*, catalogue of exhibition at the Victoria and Albert Museum, 1984

RORSCHACH Kimerly Rorschach, *The Early Georgian Landscape Garden*, catalogue of exhibition held at the Yale Center for British Art (New Haven, Connect., 1983)

SICCA 1982 (1) Cinzia Sicca, 'Burlington and Garden Design', *Lord Burlington and his Circle* (London: The Georgian Group, 1982)

SICCA 1982 (2) Cinzia Sicca, 'Lord Burlington at Chiswick: Architecture and Landscape', *Garden History*, X (1982), pp.36–69

SPENCE, OBSERVATIONS Joseph Spence, *Observations, Anecdotes and Characters of Books and Men*, ed. James M. Osborne, 2 vols. (Oxford, 1966)

SPENCE, POLYMETIS Joseph Spence, *Polymetis* (London, 1747).

TALMAN LETTERS copy of John Talman's letters from Italy, 1707–8 and 1712, The Bodleian Library MS Eng lett. e. 34

TIPPING 1924 H. Avray Tipping, 'Letters of William Kent to the Earl of Burlington', *Country Life*, LV (1924), pp. 741–2

TIPPING 1928 H. Avray Tipping, 'Four Unpublished Letters of William Kent', *Architectural Review*, LXIII (1928), pp. 180–3 and 209–11

VARDY John Vardy, *Some Designs of Mr Inigo Jones and Mr William Kent* (London, 1744)

VERTUE George Vertue, Notebook III, published in *The Walpole Society*, XXII (1934), especially pp. 139–41

VITRUVIUS BRITANNICUS Colin Campbell, then J. Badeslade and J. Rocque, *Vitruvius Britannicus*, 4 vols. (London, 1715–39)

WALPOLE *Horace Walpole: Gardenist. An edition of Walpole's 'The History of the Modern Taste in Gardening' with an estimate of Walpole's contribution to Landscape Architecture*, ed. Isabel Wakelin Urban Chase (Princeton, N.J., 1943)

WALPOLE *Horace Walpole's Correspondence*, ed. W.S. Lewis and Ralph S. Brown et al., 48 vols. (vols. 1–42, New Haven, Connect.; vols. 43–48, Oxford, 1937 et seq)

WARE Isaac Ware, *Designs of Mr Inigo Jones and others* (London, n.d., sec. ed., 1743, third ed., 1756)

WATKIN David Watkin, *The English Vision. The Picturesque in Architecture, Landscape & Garden Design* (London, 1982)

WILLIS 1978 Peter Willis, *Charles Bridgeman and the English Landscape Garden* (London, 1977)

WILLIS 1986 Peter Willis, 'The Visual Arts', in *The Context of English Literature. The Eighteenth Century*, ed. Pat Rogers (London, 1978), pp. 208–39

WILLIS Peter Willis, 'William Kent's letters in the Huntington Library, California', *Architectural History*, 29 (1986), pp. 158–167

WILSON Michael I. Wilson, *William Kent. Architect, Designer, Painter, Gardener, 1685–1748* (London, 1984)

WIMSATT W. K. Wimsatt, *The Portraits of Alexander Pope* (New Haven, Connect., 1965)

WITTKOWER 1945 Rudolf Wittkower, 'Lord Burlington and William Kent', *Archaeological Journal*, CII (1945)

WITTKOWER 1948 Rudolf Wittkower, 'The Earl of Burlington and William Kent', *York Georgian Society Occasional Papers*, 5 (1948)

WITTKOWER 1949 Rudolf Wittkower, 'Un libro di Schizzi di Filippo Juvarra a Chartsworth', *Bolletino Societa Piemontese d'Archaeologia e di Arti*, n.s. III (1949)

WITTKOWER 1974 Rudolf Wittkower, *Palladio and English Palladianism* (London, 1974)

WOODBRIDGE I Kenneth Woodbridge, 'William Kent as Landscape-Gardener. A Re-appraisal', *Apollo*, 100 (1974), pp. 126–37

WOODBRIDGE II Kenneth Woodbridge, 'William Kent's Gardening. The Rousham Letters', *Apollo*, 100 (1974), pp. 282–91

WOODBRIDGE 1981 Kenneth Woodbridge, 'Iconographic Variations: Classical and Gothic Themes in the English Landscape Garden in the Eighteenth Century', *Lotus International*, XXX (1981), pp. 11–27

WOLTERSTORFF Eric R. Wolterstorff, *British Architectural Drawings*, catalogue of exhibition held at the Yale Center for British Art (New Haven, Connect., 1982)

Notes

Introduction

1 Johnson II, p. 88

2 Vertue, pp. 139–40

3 Pope, *Correspondence*, III, 417. There is a brief and less speculative account of Kent's early life by Madeline Edmead in Hull, pp. 10–13

4 In 1709 Kent visited the Earl of Sunderland, a Secretary of State, presumably to obtain a passport (Talman letters, p. 47, dated 12 May 1709). Edmead, loc. cit., considers that Samuel Gale, an antiquary and son of the Dean of York, was the 'moving spirit' behind funding Kent's trip

5 Kent letters Lincoln, 24 November 1714

6 Middeldorf, p. 125

7 See *House in Town*, facing pp. 33 & 64; also see above, pp. 32–34

8 Kent letters Bodley, f. 4 verso

9 Kent letters Lincoln, 15 February 1717

10 See below, Chapter Three. Woodbridge I (pp. 128–9) and Sicca 1982(2) are critics who do acknowledge and discuss the debts of Kent's gardening to Italian models. See also Willis, pp. 138–9

11 On Burlington in Rome see Lees-Milne, pp. 109–10; in Genoa, Kent letters Lincoln, 15 November 1719

12 See Hunt 1986 for various accounts of how English travellers responded to Genoese gardens and grottoes

13 See Kent Journal

14 These chores are mentioned in various Kent letters Lincoln

15 Quoted Wilson, p. 30

16 On this frequent claim, see Hunt 1986, especially chapter 1

Chapter 1 Contexts for Kent's work

1 See Hunt 1986, esp. Part One, which also provides illustrations of sites seen by English tourists

2 *The Works of ... Joseph Addison* (1721), II, p. A4 verso

3 Chatsworth, Kent letters, 206.13 (24 October 1745)

4 Basil Kennett, *Romae Antiquae Notitia* (5th edition, 1713), p. 33

5 Lassels, *The Voyage of Italy* (1670), Pt. II, p. 307; anon, *A Tour in France and Italy ...* (1676), p. 92. On Lassels see Edward Chaney, *The Grand Tour and the Great Rebellion. Richard Lassels and 'The Voyage of Italy' ...* (Geneva, 1985)

6 Burnet, *Some Letters containing an account of what seemed Remarkable in Travelling through ... Italy ...* (Rotterdam, 1687), p. 215

7 Talman letters, folios 118 & 124

8 RIBA X/17

9 [William Bromley], *Remarks in the Grand Tour ... performed ... in the year 1691* (1705), p. 183

10 Wright, *Some Observations made in Travelling Through France, Italy. Etc. In the Years 1720, 1721, and 1722* (1730), II, p. 371

11 See below, cat. nos 46, 62

12 On attitudes towards antique sculpture and the fortunes of some famous items, see Francis Haskell and Nicholas Penny, *Taste and the Antique* (New Haven, Connect., 1981). On the Belvedere Villa see, amongst a large bibliography, Hans Henrik Brummer, *The Statue Court in the Vatican Belvedere* (Stockholm, 1970)

13 John Raymond, *Il Mercurio Italico ...* (1648), p. 78. For illustrations of such sculpture gardens see Hunt 1986, figures 14 & 15

14 See *The Aeneid*, Book VII

15 We know of Pope's plans from Spence, *Observations*, I, p. 257. I have discussed these in both Hunt 1983 and Hunt 1986, chapter 11

16 Kent letters Lincoln, 14 May 1713, 16 April 1715, *et passim*

17 *The Diary of John Evelyn*, ed. E. S. de Beer (Oxford, 1955), II, p. 234; *Francis Mortoft: His Book*, ed. Malcolm Letts, Hakluyt Society, sec. series, LVII (1925), pp. 124–8

18 Anon, *A Tour in France and Italy ...* (1676), p. 74

19 Spence, *Polymetis*, pp. 1 ff

20 E. Veryard, *An Account of Divers Choice Remarks ... Taken in a Journey ...* (1701), p. 193

21 Spence, *Observations*, pp. 672–7

22 Castell's reconstructed plans are by now, I think, well known: they are illustrated in Hunt 1976, plate 44, Hunt 1986, plate 99, Hunt and Willis, plate 69

23 See Hunt 1986, chapter 11. Kent mentions a visit to the villa at Poggio a Caiano (Journal, folio 3), but Wilson (pp. 26 and 202) misinterprets his reference to Pratolino as being to Poggio a Caiano

24 Spence, *Observations*, p. 250

25 For Addison, see note 2 above; otherwise, respectively, Burnet, op. cit., p. 122, J. Breval, *Remarks on Several Parts of Europe ...* (1738), p. 141, and anon, 'A True Description of ... Italy', *The Harleian Miscellany*, 12 (1811), p. 122

26 For Kent's own collection, which included some antique statues, see the *Catalogue* of the sale of his effects which took place on 13 and 14 February 1749 (Bodley: Misc Bibl.III.4°17). For his purchase of 'a fine landskip of Paul Bril' see Kent journal, folio 7 verso. For the Brill drawings discussed, see Hunt 1986, plates 20 and 21

27 See also Elaine Evans Dee, *Views of Florence and Tuscany by Giuseppe Zocchi* (New York, 1968)

28 Edmund Warcupp, *Italy in Its Originall Glory, Ruine and Revivall* (1660), II, p.195, and Wright, op. cit., p.195

29 See Hunt 1986, chapter 7

30 Veryard, op. cit., p.206

31 Wotton, *Elements of Architecture* (1624), pp.109–10

32 Moryson, *An Itinerary…* ([1617] Glasgow, 1907), p.331 and Reresby, *Memoirs* (1904), p.50

33 See Claudia Lazzaro-Bruno, 'The Villa Lante at Bagnaia: an allegory of Art and Nature', *The Art Bulletin*, LIX (1977), pp.553–660

34 John Northall, *Travels Through Italy* (1766), p.362

35 *Tour* (op. cit., note 5 above), p.78

36 Illustrated Hunt 1986, plates 97 and 98

37 See Hull, p.59

38 Dryden, *Of Dramatic Poesy and other critical essays*, ed. George Watson (1962), I, p.59

39 Mainly owing to the work of Cinzia Sicca (see Sicca 1982 (1)); but see also Lees-Milne, pp.113 ff

40 Sicca 1982(1), p.74 and Wittkower 1949

41 Kent letters Lincoln, 8 October 1716

42 Talman letters, folios 184 and 185; see also folio 232 for another theatre which Talman contrived in a *vigna*. I am grateful to Dr Terry Friedman for drawing my attention to his discussion of this in 'Foggini's Statue of Queen Anne', *Kunst des Barock in der Toskana* (Munich, 1976), pp.42 ff. For other theatre references see Kent letters Lincoln, 17 August 1712 and 26 January 1713

43 Burlington purchased designs and drawings by Jones in 1720

44 *Lord Hervey and his Friends*, ed. Lord Ilchester (1950), pp.115–16

45 See above, pp.49 ff

46 Wilson, p.178, citing E. Croft-Murray, *Decorative Painting in England 1537–1837* (1962–1970), II, p.231, for the 1724 work

47 On the pervasion of these two stage designs, see Richard Krautheimer, 'The Tragic and Comic Scene of the Renaissance', *Gazette des Beaux-Arts*, 33 (6e période, 1948), pp.327–46

48 I have outlined some of this history in my *Vauxhall and London's Garden Theatres* (Cambridge, 1985)

49 Wright (op. cit., p.316) described the 'grotta finta' in the Palazzo Altieri, Rome, as 'dispos'd in a Scene-like manner'

50 See Hunt 1986, chapter 5

51 See ibid p.72

52 We know that Nicolas Poussin used a model theatre to construct his paintings: see A. Blunt, *Nicolas Poussin* (Washington, DC, 1967), pp.242–5

53 Kent letters Lincoln, undated but summer 1714

54 Kent letters Lincoln, 24 November 1714

55 The ceilings for the Flemish church and Chicheley are illustrated in *House in Town*, facing pp.33 and 64. For his other subjects see Wilson, pp.18–19

56 Pope, *Correspondence*, I, pp.167–8. I have discussed Pope's attitudes towards the picturesque and its relation to garden design in Hunt 1985 (I)

57 The words are Félibien's of Poussin: *Entretiens* (Trévoux, 1725), p.139

58 Pope, *Poems*, VIII, 32 (being a note to Book X, line 677)

59 Ibid, VIII, 233–4 (headnote to Book XVI)

60 See Norman Bryson, *Word and Image. French painting of the Ancien Régime* (Cambridge, 1981), chapter 2

61 *The Diary of Joseph Farington*, ed. K. Cave, VIII (New Haven, Connect., 1982), p.3033

62 On Dryden and the parallel between the arts see Dean Tolle Mace, '*Ut pictura poesis*: Dryden, Poussin and the parallel of poetry and painting in the seventeenth century', *Encounters*, ed. J. D. Hunt (London, 1971), pp.58–81

63 This change in aesthetics is set out and discussed by Dean Tolle Mace, 'Transformations in classical art theory: from "poetic composition" to "picturesque composition"', *Word & Image*, I (1985), pp.59–86, from which all quotations in the following discussion are taken unless otherwise stated

64 Lines 62–64

65 The Abbé du Bos, *Critical Reflexions on Poetry, Painting, and Music*, trs. Thomas Nugent (1748)

66 *Poetry and Prose*, ed. V. A. Dearing and C. E. Beckwith (Oxford, 1974), I, p.216 (lines 53 ff.)

67 In 1685 W. Aglionby wrote that 'We never had, as yet, any of note that was an Englishman, that pretended to History Painting…', *Three Dialogues* (1685), preface

68 See Quentin Skinner, 'Meaning and Understanding in the History of Ideas', *History and Theory*, VIII (1969), pp.3–53, an essay that deserves study by all who try and 'place' Kent in gardening history

69 Woodbridge, I, p.127

70 See Ralph Cohen, *The Art of Discrimination* (1964), p.251

71 See Bradley and Eichholz in particular

72 Mason, *The English Garden* note X to Book I, line 511, in *Works* (1811). Walpole was severe about Kent's Spenser illustrations: 'the most execrable performance you ever beheld – the graving not worse than the drawing: awkward knights, scrambling Unas, hills tumbling down themselves, no variety of prospect, and three or four perpetual spruce firs…' *Correspondence*, IX (1941), p.116

73 Kent's fascination with Ovid is perhaps revealed by his ownership of a manuscript 'Breve Compendio delle Metamorfosi di Ovidio Istoricamente spiegate e descritte da GUGLIELMO KENT' (Bodley MS Rawl. D. 540). The MS is not in Kent's hand, but some annotations are (see folio 111). For the relevance of Ovid to garden design see Hunt 1986, chapter 4

74 Spence, *Observations*, pp. 19 (for Pope's early love of Spenser) and 182 (for the old lady's comment)

75 Eichholz, p.642

76 Working, as he inevitably had to, only in black and white cut Kent off from precisely the formal effects of colour that exponents of the new 'picturesque composition' promoted over subject matter

77 For instance Hogarth's (admittedly prejudiced) criticism in February 1724 with his *Masquerades and Operas* and the burlesque the following year of Kent's altarpiece for St Clement Dane's

78 Kent's journal has notes he took from two treatises on perspective by Giulio Troili, called Paradosso, and Pietro Accolti

Chapter 2 'The pencil of his imagination'

1 Walpole, p.26

2 Hull, p.7

3 Harris 1986, especially pp.143–4

4 Some one hundred and fifty years after Kent, for example, the southern terrace was laid out at Holkham by W. E. Nesfield: the only plan which does *not* survive is the one design which was implemented. I am grateful to Mr Jolly for this information

5 See Woodbridge II

6 See Tipping 1924 and Tipping 1928 for some examples of this

7 Hull, p.7. Apart from the landscape *capricci* in the catalogue below, there is an architectural *capriccio* at Chatsworth (Album 26, item 77) which shows Kent's strong vein of fantasy

8 The drawings at Chatsworth that are clearly *not* by Kent are Album 26, item 60, and Album 26A, items 63 recto and verso

9 Vertue, p.73; letter to Huntingdon, cited Wilson, p.126. Some such progress from interior decoration to garden designs occurred at Horseheath (see Hull item 50)

10 See Wittkower 1945, p.153

11 Spence, *Observations*, p.250

12 Walpole, p.26

13 See above, p.26

14 Stephen Orgel and Roy Strong, *Inigo Jones. The Theatre of the Stuart Court* (Berkeley & London, 1973), I, p.206 ff. For examples of masque language applied to gardens, see Hunt 1986, p.64

15 Orgel and Strong, op. cit., II, p.578 (and see p.588 for commentary)

16 Ibid. See also Hunt 1986, pp.115–17

17 Thomas Whately, *Observations on Modern Gardening* (1770), p.50

18 *Historical Manuscript Commission Reports*, Castle Howard MSS, VI (1897), pp.143–4

19 Southcote's remark that 'I prevailed on Kent to resume flowers in the natural way of gardening, in a natural way' (Spence, *Observations*, p.424) dates from 1752: presumably this Carlton House flower bed was early and unregenerate Kent

20 The influence of Pope's garden seems to be unquestioned (see Hull, p.6, where Twickenham is said to have provided a 'particular inspiration for Kent'). The case is not implausible, but does need arguing. Walpole on Pope's garden, *Walpole*, pp.28–9

21 Spence, *Observations*, p.253. Recently both Mack 1985 and Martin have published drawings of this obelisk done in the early nineteenth century. In the same year as Pope placed the obelisk as the culmination to his garden he commemorated his other

parent in the concluding lines of his *Epistle to Dr Arbuthnot*. His portrait by Richardson, reproduced as the frontispiece to Martin, shows the obelisk in the distance

22 Tipping 1928, p.209

23 Op. cit. (Chapter One, note 38), II, p.195

24 Hunt and Willis, p.205

25 The phrase is from a letter urging Pope to pursue his Englishing of Homer, italics mine: see Pope, *Correspondence*, I, pp.45–6. The passage is examined more fully in Hunt 1986, pp.201 ff

26 See Erwin Panofsky, 'The Ideological Antecedents of the Rolls-Royce Radiator', *Proceedings of the American Philosophical Society*, CVII (1963), pp.273–88, for a witty example of this point of view. For Shaftesbury, see his *Letter Concerning Design* (1712)

27 Kent letters Lincoln, 15 November 1718; Gwynn, *London and Westminster Improved* (1766), p.62n; Spence, *Observations*, p.409

28 Kent letters Lincoln, 30 January 1720

29 We know that Kent sent Sir John Chester drawings of the Villa Aldobrandini (called the 'Belvedere') at Frascati – Kent letters Lincoln, 16 April 1715

30 On the Elysian Fields see Clarke 1973 and Clarke 1974

31 See above chapter 1, note 42

32 Woodbridge I, p.131. On the Villa Mattei see E. MacDougall, 'The Villa Mattei & the Development of the Roman Garden Style', Harvard University Ph.D. diss., 1970

33 See Hunt 1986, plate 96

34 John Macky, *A Journey through England…* (1724), I, 61; an extract is quoted above, p.67

35 Carré 1980, pp.401–2; Lees-Milne (p.123) also cites but slightly misquotes Burlington's delight at San Giorgio Maggiore in Venice with 'an open intercolun^{on} which discovers the choire'

36 See Kent letters Lincoln, 5 November 1712

37 See Harris 1983 [p.2 of unpaginated article]; see also Hull, p.18 for details of other early gothick work. 'Gothick' has been used throughout, but without the distracting inverted commas, to designate Kent's and others' eighteenth-century versions of genuine gothic.

38 Harris 1983, [p.1]

39 Cited ibid, [p.1]

40 Kent journal, folio 7

41 Wilson, p.154

42 An eighteenth-century treatment of this important theme is Thomas Gray's poem, 'The Progress of Poetry', first published in 1757. For some discussion of the contemporary significance of Michael Drayton's celebration of the English landscape see Richard Helgerson, 'The land speaks: cartography, chorography, and subversion in Renaissance England', *Representations*, 16 (1986), 50–85, especially pp.76 ff

43 See Clarke 1973 and Michel Baridon, 'Ruins as a Mental Construct', *Journal of Garden History*, V (1985), pp.84–96. In the discussion that follows I am indebted to the latter article from which all quotations unless otherwise referenced come. I have taken these matters somewhat further in Hunt 1986, especially chapter 10

44 I argued this point in detail in my Ferens Lectures at Hull, but the catalogue of the subsequent exhibition (Hull, p.18) simply observed without elaboration that there 'is an indication that [Kent] perceived no apparent contradiction in the use of two architectural languages'

45 Cited Clarke 1973, p.568

46 See above, pp.32 ff

47 Spence, *Observations*, p.423. David Jacques half-heartedly suggests that Pope's bowling green might have been considered 'in the Great Light of a History Painting', *Garden History*, 4 (1976), p.42

48 Charles Le Brun's *Conférence sur l'expression* appeared in an English translation in 1701; on this topic see also Norman Bryson, *Word and Image* (Cambridge, 1981), chapter 2

49 See above, note 34. The Rigaud drawings are reproduced by Carré 1982

Chapter 3 Kentissime

1 Walpole, *Correspondence*, IX (1941), p.71

2 See Hassall I

3 See Colton 1974 and 1976/7, from whom all quotations are taken unless otherwise specified

4 Quoted Colton 1974, from *A Collection of Poems in Six Volumes by Several Hands* (London: Dodsley, 1758), V, 161

5 See Wilson, p.148

6 Quoted Colton 1974, p.189

7 See Baridon, 'Ruins', *Journal of Garden History*, V, 89–94

8 Kent letters Lincoln, 15 February 1717

9 The European literature is vast, but for the English scene consult Richard Foster Jones, *Ancients and Moderns; a study of the background of the Battle of the Books* (St Louis, Mo., 1936)

10 Wilson, p.155

11 Woodbridge I, p.130 and see Hunt 1986, figure 13

12 Kenelm Digby, *Observations on the 'Faerie Queene'* (1643) p.2

13 British Museum Prints and Drawings Department, 1927–7–21–6 and 9

14 See cat. no. 59

15 See Hunt 1986, figures 97 and 98

16 See Spence, *Observations*, p.415

17 In the absence of any definitive, published study of the Chiswick gardens see Clark, Carré 1973, Carré 1977 and Carré 1982 as well as Carré 1980, and Sicca 1982(2). I am also grateful to John Harris who let me see a lecture text on Chiswick's link building and the gardens

18 See above. Exactly the same emphasis occurs in early northern humanism, when Erasmus urges speaking 'in the way in which Cicero probably would speak; if he were alive, about the same matters...' quoted David Lowenthal, *The Past is a Foreign Country* (Cambridge, 1985), p.78

19 Macky, *Journey*, I, 87. Cf. Wittkower 1945, p.155, on the 'half-classicizing' effects at Chiswick

20 See Loeb Classical Library edition of Pliny's letters, letter v.6, and Castell, p.89 (also figure 36 of this book)

21 Spence, *Observations*, cf. pp.407 and 405

22 Tipping 1928, pp.180–1: it is unclear what this refers to

23 Ibid, p.182

24 I am indebted to Woodbridge I for this analysis

25 Cf. figure 39 in this book with *Vitruvius Britannicus* IV, plates 67–68 (reproduced Willis, plate 30)

26 Robert E. Wark, *Early British Drawings in the Huntington Collection* (San Marino, California, 1969), p.35

27 Willis does not comment at all on this feature of Claremont

28 See Hunt 1986, figures 41 and 83

29 See ibid, pp.85 ff

30 Whately, *Observations on Modern Gardening* (1770), pp.48–50

31 See Spence, *Observations*, p.424

32 Walpole, *Correspondence*, X, 72–3

33 Pope, *Poems*, IV, 316

34 This derivation was noted by John Martin Robinson in his review of Wilson in *AA Files no.8* (January 1985), p.109

35 Chatsworth, Album 26A, item 63 and Album 26, item 60

36 *The Seasons*, ed. James Sambrook (Oxford, 1981), p.125 (*Summer* lines 1428–31) my italics

37 See Woodbridge I where these changes of styles were first published

38 Walpole, p.29

39 Walpole, *Correspondence*, X, 72

40 Willis, pp.66–8

41 See Batey; all other unspecified quotations are from this text

42 Moggridge, p.191

43 For the latest information on Arundel's gardens see David Howarth, *Lord Arundel and his circle* (New Haven & London, 1985)

44 On the iconographical programme of the Villa D'Este see David R. Coffin, *The Villa D'Este at Tivoli* (Princeton, N.J., 1960), chapter 6. That Kent would think of the Tivoli Fountain of Ancient Rome as a 'theatre' in which representations should occur is given backing by the President de Brosses who called it a theatre: see Sicca 1982(2), p.43

45 That terraces could be interpreted as Italianate, see Hunt 1986, pp.31 and *passim*

46 See figure 39

47 Addison, *The Works* (1721), II, 131

48 See, for example, John Raymond, *Il Mercurio Italico*, p.172

49 Moggridge lists and illustrates all the surviving statuary, figures 22–26

50 This is pointed out by Moggridge, p.187

51 I made this suggestion in 'Emblem and expressionism in the 18th-century landscape garden', *Eighteenth-Century Studies*, IV (1971), pp.302–3

52 See Coffin

53 Hull p.64: 'The overall theme was that of love and death, embodied mainly by the goddess Venus in her role as *Venus genitrix*'

54 Moggridge, p.190 and figures 12 and 13

55 Pope, *Poems*, IV, 65–67

56 See above, p.92 ff

57 Pope, *Poems*, III.ii, p.142; for Pliny, letter v.6

58 See Hunt 1986, p.191 and figure 96. The antiquarian, John Loveday, thought Rousham was both antique (marbles and inscriptions) *and* 'all rural and unornamented' – see Sarah Markham, *John Loveday of Caversham 1711–1789* (Salisbury, 1984), p.375

59 Walpole, p.29

60 See above p.17 and note 31

61 Walpole, p.25

62 Ibid, p.24

63 'Meaning and understanding in the history of ideas', *History and Theory*, VIII (1969), pp.3–53

64 Walpole, p.26

65 Quoted Quaintance, p.286

66 Walpole, p.35

67 Quaintance, p.293

68 Walpole, pp.25–6

69 *Complete Body of Architecture* (1756), p.637

70 Woodbridge II, p.291

71 Spence, *Polymetis* (1747), pp.292–4 and 297

72 Reprinted in *The Renaissance Imagination* (Berkeley, California, 1975), ed. S. Orgel, pp.55–68

73 See Frank Simpson, 'Dutch paintings in England before 1760', *Burlington Magazine*, 95 (1953), pp.39–43, and Frank Herrmann, *The English as Collectors* (1972)

74 'Philanactophil' (i.e. E. Bolton), *Nero Caesar...* (1624), p.181

75 See *A Philosophical Enquiry...*, ed. J. T. Boulton (Notre Dame, Indiana, 1968), pp.lxxvii–lxxviii, 164–5 and 167–72

76 A useful commentary on these developments is Ernest Tuveson, *The Imagination as a Means of Grace: Locke and the aesthetics of Romanticism* (Berkeley, 1960)

77 *The Enthusiast* (1744), lines 4–9

78 *Polymetis*, p.290

79 Roger White, '''As finely finished as anything'': Gunnersbury Park, West London', *Country Life* (11 November, 1982), CLXXII pp.1480–2

80 Walpole, *Correspondence*, IX, 122

81 See text figures 27 and 28

82 See Robert Williams, 'Making places: garden-mastery and English Brown', *Journal of Garden History*, 3 (1983), pp.382–5

83 Walpole, *Correspondence*, XVIII, 254–55; see Hassell II

84 Tipping 1928, p.210

85 See Jacques 1983, p.32

86 John Harris, 'A note on Woburn', *Garden History*, VII/3 (1979), 11–12

87 On Worcester Lodge (and other Kent lodges) see Tim Mowl and Brian Earnshaw, *Trumpet at a Distant Gate. The lodge as prelude to the country house* (1985), pp.34–5 and *passim*

88 Walpole, *Correspondence*, XXXVII, 305 and X, 72 (at Esher Place)

89 On Wright see Eileen Harris, *Thomas Wright, Arbours & Grottoes. A facsimile, with a catalogue of Wright's works in architecture and garden design* (1980); on Robins, see John Harris, *Gardens of Delight. The English Rococo Landscape of Thomas Robins* (1979); on the influence of this particular mode of Kentian design see Dieter Hennebo, 'Tendencies in mid-18th-century German gardening', *Journal of Garden History*, V (1985), p.365

90 Richard Hurd, *Letters on Chivalry and Romance* (1762), letter 8: Hurd fails to associate the earlier 'Gothic method of design in gardening' with Kent; but, as this book argues, he could have done so and so have strengthened a finely balanced assessment.

Catalogue

The catalogue includes all Kent's known landscape sketches, together with those of his drawings for garden and park buildings and a few others which are usefully considered in that connection; this includes such of his designs for Spenser's *The Faerie Queene* that employ important landscape features.

Since the dating of Kent's sketches is extremely speculative, not to say impossible in most cases, the present catalogue lists them according to their location (in the case of London, alphabetically by museum or gallery under the London entry); drawings in private locations otherwise unspecified are grouped at the end. Abbreviations used are those listed in the bibliography. All measurements are in centimetres, height before width.

Buildings &c for Mount.

1

A   B

2

BADMINTON, GLOUCESTERSHIRE
(N.B. since all these drawings were seen while on deposit at the Gloucestershire Record Office, GRO references are given. The drawings have since returned to Badminton)

1 Sketch for mount, Badminton
21 × 29.6
Pen and wash over traces of pencil
Glos RO 4/13
LIT: Colvin 1968, figure 13

Inscribed bottom right 'Buildings &c for Mount'. Perhaps about 1745. The proposal shows a rectangular body of water at right angles to the viewer on the left; at centre an archway with flanking urns gives upon the mount, up which a clearing among trees leads towards an octagonal (or hexagonal) roofed temple.

2 Sketches for Badminton
29.6 × 43
Pen and ink wash over pencil in parts
Glos RO 4/11; Badminton Portfolio
    Architectural Drawings (vol: House
    & Gardens), item 1
LIT: Colvin 1968, figure 14

The recto (shown here) contains two designs: at left a bridge over water with a grotto at its head, marked 'A'; at right, marked 'B', a gothick, ogive-arched seat in a copse. The verso (not illustrated) has a design for an alcove in the park walls and annotations for the recto sketches: 'Arch [sic] & accompaniment for the Ends of Water on the Lawn', and 'A romantic Seat for a small Piece of Water in the Forest Part of Park'. Again, probably about 1745. The left-hand sketch is clearly Kent's, a proposal for the park adjacent to the north side of the house that a few years later was painted by Canaletto (see 57), though this is no guarantee that the scheme was effected; the right-hand one is in a different scale entirely, and stylistically is more sophisticated in its handling of foliage than Kent usually is.

3 Sketch for bridge over water
No details survive

This is a large scale version of the bridge shown in the 'A' sketch of cat. no. 2 and in Canaletto's view from the north front: annotated 'the Arches crossing the Head of the intended lower water' and with scale. It was a drawing discovered at Badminton in the 1960s by Mr Howard Colvin, but since lost. Only a xerox (reproduced here) survives.

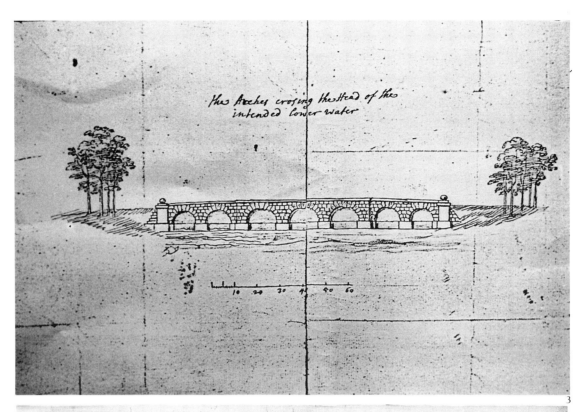

3

4 'Buildings on Lawn', Badminton
21 × 29
Ink and wash over pencil

Inscribed in the same hand as cat. no. 1. This shows Kent attempting to control a larger area than his usual commissions entailed. In the far distance we see Kent's handsome Worcester Lodge, but without its accompanying screen of walls to either side; a grotto at the head of some water is to the left, rather different from that designed in cat. nos 2 and 3 and shown by Canaletto; a rotunda of a familiar Kentian model in a grove of trees at right; its groundplan drawn below; in the far distance at the right a version of the pavilion drawn in cat. no. 1. Between are the huge spaces which must have made Badminton such a different design proposition for Kent.

4

5

5 Proposal for north lawn at Badminton
dimensions not recorded
Faint pencil
Glos RO 4/9

Exceptionally faint sketch undoubtedly
by Kent of the whole area later
represented by Canaletto: annotated
'A Sketch for the Lawn at Badminton'.
On the bottom left is shown the cascade
at the head of the water (see cat. nos 1
and 2), on right both the temple of cat.
no. 4 and a mount much more smooth
and perfectly circular and crowned
with a different temple than in cat.
no. 1 and with a different, more
baroque archway. It also suggests in
the network of lines that Kent was
working to keep the criss-cross
hunting avenues shown in Johannes
Kip's bird's-eye view – a format which
is unique to Kent and which was
presumably forced upon him by
having to consider the design of such
a vast site.
Not photographed while at Gloucester
Record Office; no longer accessible at
Badminton (photograph from xerox).

CHATSWORTH, DERBYSHIRE
*The Trustees of the Chatsworth
Settlement*

6

6 Hilly landscape, with river god,
large building and dog's head
23.7 × 18.6
Pen and sepia ink over pencil
Chatsworth Album 26, item 12 verso
LIT: Hull item 20, where dated
  'c. 1738–40'

Probably a *capriccio*, though it could
be related to Kent's other ideas for the
Chatsworth hillside (cf. cat. nos 16, 17,
18, 21 and 22). The large nine-bay
building in the background is 'very
strongly reminiscent of Kent's project
for the Duke of Grafton's seat at
Euston, Suffolk' (Hull). The
disproportionate head of a dog is a
typical piece of Kentian whimsey,

7

8

while the river god recalls Italianate imagery.

7 Chiswick birdhouse, with round pond and fountain; woman feeding birds; a man with broom, and a kennel
19.5 × 18.5
Pen
Chatsworth 26, item 25a

8 Obelisk and archway at Chiswick
19.4 × 14.5
Pen
Chatsworth 26, item 25b

9 Dog, cat and birds before Chiswick birdhouse
18.2 × 22
Pen and wash
Chatsworth 26, item 25
Cf. cat. no. 7

9

10a

10a Alexander Pope in his grotto
22 × 18.5
Pen and brown wash over pencil
Chatsworth 26, item 39 recto
LIT: Wimsatt, plate 15; Boutwood,
    figure 3; Mack 1969, plate 26;
    Apollo of the Arts, item 65; Hunt
    1976, plate 31; Brownell, plate 55;
    Hunt 1983, plate 14; Hull item 31;
    Mack 1985, plate 44

10b Rough sketches of grotto layout,
vaults and vista through tunnel
Chatsworth 26, item 39 verso

Sometimes attributed to Lady
Burlington or Kent (Mack 1969), it
seems likely that it must be Kent's.
Usually dated to the end of the 1720s
(Brownell, Mack 1985), the Hull
catalogue puts it 'c.1740–41' on the
basis of an assumption that pillars were
added during Pope's reworking of the
grotto in 1740: but his letter to Borlase
(*Correspondence*, IV, 246) does not state
conclusively that the pillars were new

additions, indeed it rather implies that groins were added to existing pillars. But on these grounds Hull argues that the verso sketches are Kent's suggestions ('in the middle of a party at Chiswick') for Pope's new grotto works, and the recto a 'later' version of what the new grotto interior would look like. The grotesques at the top of the recto – a butterfly and, to its right, earlier stages of its development from chrysalis – may be an allusion to Pope's jest about the 'maggot Muse' (*Dunciad* (1742), I, 61); they convey in any case Kent's playful response to his friend's equally fantastical concept of the grotto and its centrality in his poetical reputation and iconography..

10b

11 Pope in his grotto
12.1 × 16.6
Pen and brown wash over pencil
Chatsworth 26, item 51
LIT: *TLS*, 7 April 1961; Wimsatt, plate
    16; Mack 1969, plate 15; Hull item
    30

Like cat. no. 10a, this has also been attributed to Lady Burlington (Mack 1969), but with no substantial authority; so Kent remains a strong candidate on stylistic grounds above all. Compared with cat. no. 10a this view exaggerates the wide, scenographic character of Pope's grotto (it could never have had such width), perhaps in deference to the poet's own theatrical claims for his Twickenham retreat (see Hunt 1985, p. 93). The lamp burning above Pope's head is presumably that of 'thin Alabaster' (*Correspondence*, II, 297).

11

12

14

12 Cuttle Mill, Rousham, Oxfordshire: sketch of elevation and part of ground plan
20.6 × 18.5
Pen over pencil
Chatsworth 26, item 56
LIT: Woodbridge I, plate 6; Woodbridge II, plate 6; Hull item 36

This sketch makes a feature of an existing building on the other side of the River Cherwell from the gardens at Rousham by giving it a gothick front; this heightening of an indigenous building, making it participate in the overall scheme at Rousham, is discussed above p.87. General Dormer's gardener, John MacClary, refers to the building as 'the Gothick Corn Mill' (Batey, p.129).

13

13 Park landscape, with donkey pulling farmcart, accompanied by lady riding side-saddle on a horse; large urn in semi-circular grove behind. Girl's head drawn in bottom right margin
20.3 × 31.2
Pen and brown wash over pencil
Chatsworth 26, item 58
LIT: Willis, plate 175b

14 Four chickens hanging a fox in front of the Chiswick Aviary
20.2 × 18.8
Pen and wash over pencil
Chatsworth 26, item 83
LIT: Hull item 18

Two chickens pulling ropes, one standing and one in tree together with an owl; lady pleading with chickens. Verso has verses in Pope's hand on the Twickenham grotto (see *Poems*, VI, 382–5, which does not, however, mention this MS version at Chatsworth).

Interesting for its suggestion of Kent's humour (Hull suggests that the scene alludes to an incident in the Burlington family of 1736), the drawing is more important as confirming the elevation of the Chiswick Aviary represented by John Rocque in a marginal vignette on his 1726 plan of the gardens.

15 Sea-horse pavilion: elevation and siting
35 × 48.7
Chalk and washes
Chatsworth 20, item 121

Perhaps a project for Chiswick (to terminate the Grande Allée). The most baroque of Kent's designs; but the right-hand sketch of how the pavilion would look is typical of his interest in setting and in the viewer's perspective (here rather dramatically heightened).

15

16 Octagonal or hexagonal pavilion on a wooded hillside beside a cascade
18 × 30
Pen and ink; marked with D-Dev
    (Devonshire)
Chatsworth album 26A, item 2

This, the two following drawings and perhaps cat. nos 6, 21 and 22 all represent projects for re-structuring the hillside at Chatsworth, the scale of which was much larger than Kent generally attempted. His various projects focus around the already existing Great Cascade, which is first given a more natural aspect and then associated with temples in the manner of the famous Aniene Cascades and so-called Sybil's Temple at Tivoli (see text no. 9). The building here is similar to the building proposed for the top of the mount at Badminton (cat. no. 1).

16

17

17 Round temple on hillside with
cascade
18.6 × 26
Pen and ink
Chatsworth 26A, item 3
LIT: Woodbridge 1981, plate 22

Another projection for the Chatsworth
hillside, this time invoking a version
of the so-called Sybil's Temple or
Temple of Vesta at Tivoli, which Kent
was to use for the Temple of Ancient
Virtue at Stowe in the 1730s.

18 Proposal for the hillside at
Chatsworth
50.5 × 32
Sepia ink and wash over pencil
Chatsworth 26A, item 4
LIT: Woodbridge I, figure 4; Blunt 124;
     Hunt 1983, plate 6; Hull item 46;
     Hunt 1986, figure 104

The most elaborate of surviving
proposals for the Chatsworth hillside,
this is an anthology of Kent's favourite
Italianate themes – the round temple
from Tivoli, cascades from the upper
gardens of the Villa Aldobrandini at
Frascati (also invoked by Kent at
Chiswick and Rousham) and twin
temples surmounted by pyramids;
these last are based on an 'illustration
of the Temple of Fortune in the
Hyperotomachia Poliphili' (sic) of 1499
(Hull, p.74). See above, p.51

18

19

19 Outcrop of rock with two soldiers
18.8 × 31.4
Pen and ink, wash, over pencil
Chatsworth 26A, item 5

This and the following drawing
feature outcrops of rock in the manner
of Salvator Rosa; in this drawing are
added two soldiers even more
reminiscent of some Rosa scenes.
Kent's friend and patron at Holkham,
Thomas Coke, owned a fine Rosa
picture (see *Treasure Houses of Britain*
catalogue [Washington DC 1985], item
312) and Kent himself owned at least
one Rosa painting which was engraved
and published by Pond in the 1740s.

20

20 Outcrop of rock with pine trees
22.9 × 27.35
Pen and ink, wash, over pencil
Chatsworth 26A, item 6

This, especially the trees, is more
clearly in Kent's hand than the
preceding. It suggests how much his
prime concern was with specific areas
or even items in a garden or landscape
provided with their scenic, even
theatrical, context (here another Rosa
frisson).

21 Sloping landscape with outline of
pool and two water pavilions
32.4 × 41.4
Pen and ink and brown wash over
    pencil
Chatsworth 26A, item 7
LIT: Woodbridge I, plate 16; Willis,
    plate 176a

Perhaps a sketch for the Chatsworth
hillside (at left) with the outline of the
canal pool dotted in; the far hemicycle
with twin pavilions anticipates Kent's
first ideas for the mount at Holkham,
also linked (though in a different disposition) with water – see cat. no. 50.

21

22

22 Domed temple with three-arch portico before a rectangular pool of water with wooded hillside behind
48.8 × 35
Pen and ink and brown wash over
    pencil
Chatsworth 26A, item 8
LIT: Woodbridge I, plate 3; Willis,
    plate 172b; Hull item 47

Another sketch for the Chatsworth hillside, this time making a more prominent feature of a Roman temple and *piscina*, on the edge of which are posed two (?antique-like) bathers; Hull catalogue rightly suggests the Poussinesque tone which these bathers give to the design. The geometry of façade and pool edges may be ascribed to Kent's sensitivity to the need for regularity near a house.

23 Entrance to Chiswick House from the south west
25.9 × 35.8
Pen and ink and brown wash over
    pencil
Chatsworth 26A, item 12
LIT: Jourdain, plate 5; *Apollo of the Arts*, item 73; Blunt, 122A; Wilson, plate 22

A record of the entrance façade of Kent's patron's neo-palladian villa, angled so as to give prominence to the statue of Andrea Palladio by Rysbrack. The two men are accompanied by one of Kent's habitual, mischievous dogs.

23

24 View through the southern portico of Chiswick House from the east
29.2 × 37.2
Pen and ink and brown wash over
    pencil
Chatsworth 26A, item 13
LIT: *Apollo of the Arts*, item 74

Similar to previous item, this time taken at right angles to the entrance axis; statue of Inigo Jones.

24

25

25 Classical design for cascade at Chiswick, with coach and horses approaching
33.4 × 49
Pen and brown wash over pencil
Chatsworth 26A, item 15

One of several attempts to provide a suitable headpiece for the river at Chiswick; the severe classical design seems to be echoed by the geometry of the pool's edges. A cascade in classical style would have been an apt addition to the antique tone of Chiswick; eventually it was erected in a 'natural' style but with clear allusions to modern Italy (see above pp.68 ff).

26

26 Rustic cascade at Chiswick, with state coach departing towards right
35.6 × 47.1
Pen and ink and brown and grey
    washes over pencil
Chatsworth 26A, item 16
LIT: Hull item 16

An angled view of the cascade, seen from east bank of the river, now rustically designed in the manner of Kent's preferred model at the Villa Aldobrandini, Frascati; the classical imagery is still retained in the urn. The edges of the pool seem now to be 'natural', but the vegetation behind the cascade less thick.

27 Obelisk and arch at Chiswick by
moonlight
29.8 × 37.2
Brown ink and wash over pencil
Chatsworth 26A, item 17
LIT: *Apollo of the Arts*, item 76; Carré
    1980, figure 34

Perhaps something of a *capriccio*, since
the obelisk (with its bas-relief of a
marble formerly in the Arundel
Collection, only hinted at if at all in
this drawing) and the arch (by Inigo
Jones, bought from Sir Hans Sloane
and moved to Chiswick in 1738) could
not be seen together in this way. Some
typically Kentian whimsey in the
sleeping man and rabbits (or are they
foxes?) dancing in a ring with a dog
approaching from the right.

27

28 Design for partly rustic cascade
18.5 × 23.7
Pen over pencil
Chatsworth 26A, item 18

Probably another stab at the Chiswick
cascade, this time obviously a rapid
sketch with a few of the usual Kentian
fill-ins to form a backdrop. The upper
section of the cascade is rustic, but
only just, as the rough stones follow
the rhythms of the classical openings
at the water-level below; a severe ramp
leads the driveway across.

28

29

29 Design for a rustic cascade
35.6 × 47.1
Pen and ink and washes over pencil
Chatsworth 26A, item 19
LIT: Wittkower 1945, plate VIII/2;
    Lees-Milne, facing p.146; *Apollo of
    the Arts*, item 77; Woodbridge I,
    plate 6; Wittkower 1974, plate 156;
    Blunt, figure 122c; Hull item 17

This is another attempt at the
Chiswick cascade, and it is the image
used by Rocque as a vignette on his
1736 plan of the gardens. It dispenses
on this occasion with the driveway
across the front, but seems to supply a
pathway over the top. The arches of
rough stones and the falls of water
within the arches recall his solution
later for the Vale of Venus at
Rousham. The setting, especially the
bank cutting into the view from the
left, is irregular and in keeping with
the design of the cascade (it lacks a
pediment in this design). The Hull
catalogue compares the stonework in
this design with Kent's tailpiece for
Pope's *Odyssey* XI (1725–26).

30

30 Chiswick obelisk with archway
behind, with man and dog urinating
35.5 × 29.3
Pen and ink and brown wash over
    pencil
Chatsworth 26A, item 20
LIT: Wilson, plate 76

The obelisk is shown here without the
bas-relief (cf. cat. no. 27). The world
of ancient art, prominent in the two
architectural features is wittily called
in question by the claims of nature
possessing alike modern man and
beast.

31 Lake scene by moonlight (or with setting sun)
23 × 36.7
Pen and ink and brown wash over
  pencil
Chatsworth Album 26A, item 21
LIT: Willis, plate 173b; Willis 1978,
  plate 29; Wilson, 84; Hull item 19

This has been distantly modelled upon one of Inigo Jones's masque settings in Burlington's collection (see Stephen Orgel and Roy Strong, *Inigo Jones. The Theatre of the Stuart Court* (London, 1973), II, plates 383 and 384 rather than plate 401 suggested by Hull catalogue). Kent's drawing might, in fact, be a stage design: see text above, p.30. Hull catalogue unconvincingly suggests that this is both a design 'possibly for Claremont' and 'a view of Claremont, taken from the shore of the island, upwards towards the semicircle of trees on the side of the hill to the right of the amphitheatre'; in support of this second suggestion is cited Rocque's 1738 plan of Claremont with 'an identical layout of trees'.

31

32 Side view of Chiswick House, with top of Venus Column behind; man walking with dog
27.1 × 22.15
Pen and ink and brown wash over
  pencil
Chatsworth 26A, item 22

33 Venus column, Chiswick, with a peacock
28.8 × 23.4
Pen and ink and brown wash over
  pencil
Chatsworth 26A, item 23
LIT: Carré 1980, plate 30

32

33

34

34 Design for exedra, Chiswick, with four figures
33 × 51.5
Pen and brown and grey washes over pencil
Chatsworth 26A, item 24
LIT: Wittkower 1945, plate IX/1; Woodbridge I, plate 10; Wittkower 1974, plate 157; Hunt 1976, plate 41 (detail); Willis, figure 174b; Sicca 1982(2), plate 23; Woodbridge 1981, plate 18; Wilson, plate 77; Hull item 13

This proposal to replace the quincunx grove to the north of the villa was rejected, perhaps because of its false scale (too dominant architecture), and was reused as the Temple of British Worthies at Stowe (see cat. no. 109). At the left is a characteristic Kent device – a temple glimpsed through a transparent barrier of trees. As in many of Kent's finished drawings, the scene is peopled. For a discussion of the central feature with busts and pyramidal centre see above pp.51ff.

35

35 Revised version of exedra, Chiswick
30 × 54.3
Faint pencil
Chatsworth 26A, item 25

A wide-angled view of the proposal for the Chiswick exedra that was finally adopted. In contrast to the following item, which is suggested as a commemorative drawing, this faint pencil draft may be a design *essai*. There are no figures to suggest the scale. According to Defoe's *Tour* (1742), p.289, the statues representing Caesar, Pompey and Cicero had come from Hadrian's Villa. Hull catalogue proposes an interesting iconography for this section of Burlington's garden in 1733.

36 View into the exedra at Chiswick
29 × 40.3
Pen and ink and brown wash over
    pencil
Chatsworth 26A, item 26
LIT: Wittkower 1945, plate IX/2;
    Jourdain, figure 6; Hussey, plate 24;
    Apollo of the Arts, item 75;
    Wittkower 1974, plate 158; Hunt
    1976, plate 42; Blunt, figure 122b;
    Willis, plate 58a; Wilson, plate 78;
    Hull item 14

Compared with the preceding item,
this seems more likely to be a
commemoration of the exedra rather
than a design for it; in the background
is glimpsed the Venus Column; three
dogs prance across this 'arena'.

36

37 Front view of exedra, Chiswick
17.6 × 28.3
Faint pencil

A slightly more widely angled view of
cat. no. 35.

37

38

38 Chiswick gardens, with obelisk, arch and a departing coach
32.1 × 48.9
Pencil and brown wash
Chatsworth 26A, item 37
LIT: Carré 1980, figure 33

A very quick sketch, suggesting Kent's ability to visualise alternative prospects from one spot in a landscape.

39

39 Alternative design for the Orangery, Chiswick
27.2 × 47.1
Pen and brown wash over pencil
Chatsworth 26A, item 38

Cf. Rigaud's drawing of the Orangery reproduced Carré 1982, figure 4.

40 Design for rustic cascade with temple behind
27.4 × 38.3
Pen over pencil
Chatsworth 26A, item 39
LIT: Hull item 15

Another attempt at the Chiswick cascade, though this time the stonework is formed more evenly with the central segment bearing a pointed pediment; the carriageway is clearly shown passing across the front; but *pace* the Hull catalogue which says it is 'exactly the same' as that in cat. no. 26 above, the scale of this one is smaller. The temple behind to the right on a hill would not have been feasible on such a flat site as Chiswick, and is perhaps a *capriccio* element. It anthologises the temples projected in cat. nos 17 and 18 for the Chatsworth hillside to produce what looks like a semicircular temple with a semi-octagonal roof, a round-arched niche in the interior.

40

41 Ponds in woodland groves
30.6 × 41.6
Pen and brown wash over pencil
Chatsworth 26A, item 43
LIT: Willis, plate 173a; Woodbridge I, plate 19; Woodbridge 1981, figure 21; Hunt 1985 (II), figure 3

There appear to be one, even two ponds beyond that in the immediate foreground; they could also perhaps be clearings since Kent shows reflections only in the first. Perhaps this is a stage design rather than a project for some actual landscape.

41

42

45

43

42 Design for base of statue of the Dying Gladiator, Rousham, Oxfordshire
30.2 × 24.2
Pen and brown wash over pencil
Chatsworth 26A, item 51
LIT: Woodbridge II plate 9

The ground plan marked with length – '6 ft 9 in'. Erected above the Praeneste Terrace in 1741, the statue may have alluded to Rousham's owner, General Dormer, then very ill. The sarcophagus base in this drawing emphasises the *color romanus* of the garden item; but, as it survives today, the statue is on a simple rectangular stone base.

43 Floral temple and round pool
25 × 35.5
Pen and brown wash over pencil
Chatsworth 26A, item 70
LIT: Willis, plate 172a; Sicca 1982(2), plate 21; Wilson, plate 74; Hull item 12

Hull catalogue suggests that this is a design of 1730–3 for the flower garden south-west of the canal at Chiswick, with which Lady Burlington is supposed to have concerned herself; Hull identifies the second figure as James Cambridge, her servant. If this drawing does represent that flower garden, then the top of the archway showing above the little temple is a *capriccio* element. Wilson suggests that the drawing represents 'the original source' for or 'an early version' of the Orangery design (pp. 191–2). The columns of the charming little temple feature Vitruvius's suggestion that pillars had their origin in trees, and this idea is extended in the festoons of greenery on the temple front. The idea of a garden in front of a temple (or, conversely, a temple as a garden pavilion) probably derives from the happenstance of Rome as Kent saw it; it was a juxtaposition used elsewhere at Chiswick for the Tempietto.

44 Birdhouse at Chiswick; pool with a couple in a boat, the woman fishing
27.6 × 22.7
Pen and brown wash over pencil
Chatsworth 26A, item 71
LIT: Woodbridge I, plate 18; Woodbridge 1981, plate 17

A different representation of the aviary than that in Rocque's engravings of Chiswick; this incorporates a favourite mannerist delight of Kent in pillars transformed into herms (cf. his design for the Holkham seat, cat. nos 51 and 53). This is another distinctive example of his opening views from one part of a garden to another via thin screens of trees.

45 Temple, herms, statue of lion in a grove, with a man and a lady and a negro servant bearing drinks on a tray
34.8 × 26.2
Pen and brown wash over pencil
Chatsworth 26A, item 72
LIT: Willis, plate 174a; Wilson, plate 79

Possibly a Chiswick scene. A Kent letter of 1738 talks of 'Piedestals for the Lions' in the gardens there (Tipping 1928, p.182).

44

46

47

46 *Capriccio* landscape with a harbour
36.4 × 54.1
Pen and brown wash over pencil
Chatsworth 26A, item 74
LIT: Willis, plate 176b; Wilson, plate
83; Hull item 10

This 'extraordinarily jumbled and crowded drawing', says Wilson (p. 207); but presumably, since Kent is rarely that in his landscape designs, this is part of its joke – a humorous version of his nevertheless habitual love of allusion. In this instance Kent has assembled Trajan's Column, Titus's Arch, a minuscule Coliseum, the Pont du Gard at Nîmes, a composite circular temple (partly from Rome, partly from Tivoli), a version of Palladio's design for the Rialto Bridge. The harbour scene is Claudian, and the two helmeted figures at the bottom left leaning against a piece of fallen masonry Rosa-like. In contrast to this assemblage of art, a volcano erupts in the rear and a natural cascade tumbles down a wild hillside to form a wing on the right.

47 Theatre design
31.5 × 48.5
Pencil
Chatsworth Drawings IX, folio 80, item
117
LIT: *The Walpole Society Annual Volume*, XII (1924), pp. 155–8;
Hunt 1985 (II), plate 2

Clearly a Kent drawing, but since it is bound at the end of a volume of theatre designs at Chatsworth it has escaped the attention of landscape historians. Hunt (II) 1985 first claimed that, since its inclusion in such a volume argues that it was a design for a stage set, we might wish to reconsider such items as cat. no. 31 which could be theatre as much as landscape designs. In this case Kent invokes some of his favourite effects – temples glimpsed through open screens of trees – with a curving pond, on which he has drawn a stately regatta (perhaps a reminiscence of his visit to Venice);

the largest boat bears a slight resemblance to his own design for the royal barge with (wittily) a central pavilion modelled on Palladio's Villa Rotunda.

EUSTON HALL, SUFFOLK
His Grace the Duke of Grafton

48 Design for the park at Euston, with distant triumphal arch
21.6 × 51.4
Pen and wash over pencil
LIT: *Country Life*, CXXI (24.i.57), plate 9; Hussey, plate 227; Woodbridge I, plate 14; Hull item 22

As with the following drawing, Kent is required to work here on a large expanse of parkland; though this does not spoil his appetite for disproportionate huntsmen, barges on a recently serpentined river, and country carts and carriages. On the basis of a letter from Kent to Burlington about visiting the work in progress (see Tipping, p. 209), Hull dates this late 1737. Avenues of trees have been removed (see Arthur Oswald's three essays on Euston in *Country Life*, January 1957), and trees clumped on the slopes above the river; others frame the triumphal arch-like theatrical wings; the arch was built as a rotunda with gate lodges not shown on this drawing. At Euston in 1743 Walpole disparaged 'Kent's passion, clumps – that is, sticking a dozen trees here and there, till a lawn looks like a ten of spades' (*Correspondence*, 18 (1955), 254–5).

49 Project for new house and eastern park, Euston
33.2 × 52.1
Pen and brown wash over pencil
LIT: *Country Life*, CXXI (24.i.57), plate 2; Hussey, plate 228; Woodbridge I, plate 13; Watkin, p. 27; Woodbridge 1981, plate 26; Hull item 21

The house, with which the Duke of Grafton wanted to replace an old-

48

49

50

51

fashioned one in 1731, was never built. From the gondola on the foreground water to the temple on the horizon, the palladian house with its wide embrace of wings and the disproportionate deer, this is purely Kentian, though unusual in that he is required to think of a large area of ground. The remains of old avenues (see previous item) are retained towards the brow of the hill. The parish church is shown at extreme right.

HOLKHAM HALL, NORFOLK
The Earl of Leicester

50 Holkham Hall, proposal for a seat on the mount
37.7 × 30
Pen and wash over pencil
LIT: Hussey, plate 27; Woodbridge I, plate 22; Woodbridge 1981, plate 28; Hull item 40

Dated 'before 1733' by Woodbridge I; this proposal created an amphitheatre-like space within the arms of a curving topiary tunnel which has a pair of stone entrance portals which echo the imagery of the central seat itself. The seat was eventually built (see cat. no. 53) but without the other Italianate structures – see above, p.79. The mount lies to the south-west of the Hall and can still be registered as a swelling in the ground; on the left of this drawing is shown the western pavilion on the south lawn overlooking a rectangular pool of water. The topiary tunnel with an entrance guarded by herms is a device used by Kent in his Gay illustrations (see 45, p. 78).

51 Rough draft of elements of previous item
37 × 29
Pen and wash

This shows one half of the topiary tunnel, with suggestions of stepped sides to the amphitheatre, the central seat and one of the topiary tunnel entrances. The treatment of the descending levels of the amphitheatre, with cypress trees at regular intervals, recalls various Italian designs as well as the area in front of the Chiswick Tempietto.

52 Holkham Hall, design for the south lawn
28.9 × 49.5
Pen and wash
LIT: Woodbridge I, plate 21; Hull item 41

Dated by Woodbridge I 'before 1733'. Hull comments that it is 'somewhat surprising to find such a formal treatment of the water as well as such a rigid alignment of the pavilions'. But this is not unknown in Kent's oeuvre (see cat. no. 22) and has supposedly antique and certainly modern Italian precedents with which Coke and Kent would have been familiar; this design, unlike cat. no. 50, was executed and one of the pavilions still shows in the reformulated mount scheme (see next).

53 Holkham Hall, revised design for a seat on the mount
28.9 × 50
Pen and wash
LIT: Hussey, plate 26; Wittkower 1974, plate 209; Woodbridge I, plate 23

Dated 'before 1743' by Woodbridge I; this is a revised and more natural version of that in cat. no. 50, and for a full discussion of its significance see above p.79. The scene is decorated with apt country events – a lady fishing from a boat and a gentleman driving a gig – and is perhaps part of Kent's attempt to maintain some Italian significance within an intrinsically English prospect. The seat was built, but dismantled in the nineteenth century; the caryatids flanking the opening were given away early in the twentieth century and now decorate a cottage front (59, p. 98) nearby at Burnham Overy Town; Kent shows a similar feature on the Chiswick aviary (cat. no. 44).

52

53

54

54 Holkham Hall, sketch of lawn, with clumps of trees and a distant entry lodge
29 × 53
Pen and (?) wash
LIT: Hussey, plate 226 (though labelled as for Euston); von Buttlar, figure 28; Jacques 1983, plate 13

Such clumps were disparaged by Walpole (see cat. no. 48); but they do allow Kent to have 'natural' elements which yet alert visitors to the contrivance of the whole; here they also form a deep stage-like central glade.

55

55 Holkham Hall, triumphal arch with donkey
31.3 × 50.5
Ink and wash
LIT: Wittkower 1945, plate X/1; Jourdain, plate 3; Lees-Milne, plate facing p.256; Wittkower 1974, plate 159; Hull item 39

Inscribed in Kent's handwriting 'W. Kent/Lord Leicester', and therefore the inscription presumably dates from post-1744 when Thomas Coke, Lord Lovell became the Earl of Leicester. The drawing is dated by Hull 'before 1733'. The Triumphal Arch, along with the Obelisk and the Temple in the woods, were the first items designed for the gardens at Holkham, which were started in the late 1720s before the building of the Hall and when the idea was clearly to give the park an antique cast. The arch is situated over two miles south of the house on a hill that looks down the Obelisk avenue. An unusual, very Kentian fantasy, with allusions to Roman pyramids and (noted by Wittkower 1945) to Vanbrugh's archways at Castle Howard.

56 Holkham Hall, design for obelisk
44.8 × 24.9
Pen and wash

Another of the early designs for the
park; the annotations are by Thomas
Coke. It was erected in a circular
amphitheatrical clearing among the
ilexes, themselves – as the classical
oak tree – another classicising touch
(see Hassell I).

57 Hermitage for Richmond
22.9 × 18.8
Pen and brown ink
LIT: Hull, item 11; Sicca, '"Like a
  shallow cave by nature made":
  William Kent's natural architecture
  at Richmond', *Architectura*, vol. 16,
  1986, pp.68–82

Recently discovered at Holkham by
Cinzia Sicca, this is the only known
drawing by Kent of this important
early project (see Colton 1974 and
above, pp.62–5); '16ft' is inscribed in
Kent's handwriting within the octagon
of the groundplan. This is evidently a
preliminary sketch ('perhaps drawn at
the dinner table' says Hull) and the
building was altered and improved
before completion.

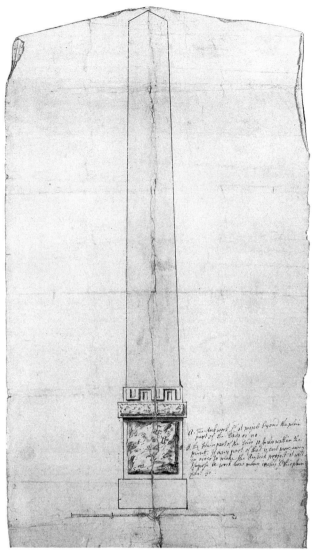

56

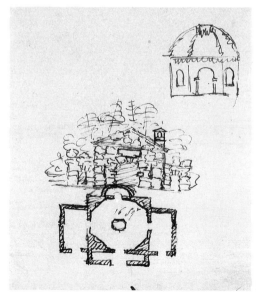

57

58

58 Fireplace with *capriccio* landscape for Holkham
34 × 22
Pen and wash

One of many designs for interior decoration, but included here to show Kent's facility with classical *capricci*, including in its cut-off pyramid a version of the Monument to Congreve at Stowe. The oval was in the end filled by a mosaic reputedly from Hadrian's Villa, which gave the required *color romanus* far more authentically.

LINCOLN
Lincolnshire Archives Office

59 Sketch plan of a summerhouse
Letter from Kent to Burrell Massingberd, 'Rome October ye 12 1715'

Massingberd, one of Kent's patrons during his Italian years, wrote to seek his help with 'both architecture & painting [i.e. decoration]' (27 June 1715 written on Kent's of 16 April 1715). In this letter of 12 October Kent responds, welcoming Massingberd's having 'become a convert to ye Italian gusto in Building' and asking for more information along the lines of his sketch which suggests how to show niches ('neaches'). This is the earliest surviving 'design' for a garden building from Kent's hand.

59

LONDON
British Museum

60 Drawing of view from terrace at Claremont, with annotations for alterations ('a Johns level terras to be taken away' on bottom left; 'fronting ye great room' on bottom right; 'ye stable road' and 'path sunk' in middle distance)
24 × 34
Pen and ink
Department of Prints and Drawings (1962−7−14−50)
LIT: Hussey, plate 29; *House in Town*, p.93

The view is presumably that from the east end of the house looking over the terrace: see J. Rocque's *Survey of the House, Gardens and Park… [at Claremont]* (1750). The reference on the sketch is undoubtedly to work by Sir John Vanbrugh. This is a unique sketch among Kent's surviving drawings in that it contains instructions to workmen on what alterations to make in the garden and landscape or Kent's own memoranda.

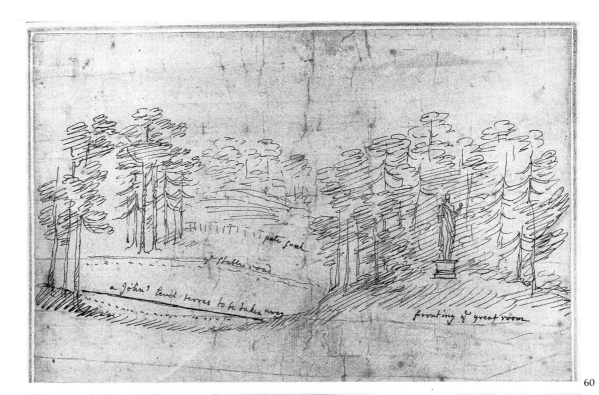

60

61 Woodland grove with two herms
24 × 34
Pen and wash over some pencil
Department of Prints and Drawings (1962−7−14−48)
LIT: Willis, plate 175a; Woodbridge I, plate 12; Hull item 28; Hunt 1985, plate 4

Typical of Kent's interest in specific, scenic moments in larger landscapes. The herms are garlanded. This is perhaps a sketch for a stage setting; at any rate it could serve equally as a stage set or a theatre in an actual grove. Hull, without explanation, describes this as 'an alternative solution for the rearrangement of trees and statuary on the hillock immediately facing the Great Room at Claremont'.

61

Hampton
court
he meets the soft
and gentle Mole
Homes Dale
raised hills

mole digs his
self a path

the ocean doth
return

James under-
stood what
pains the
Mole
did take

the ocean doth return,
and thrusteth in the Tide,
up towards the place, where first his much loved Mole was seen.
& ever since doth flow, beyond delightful Sheen

62

62 Landscape *capriccio* with
Hampton Court, Esher and river
scene with triton
17 × 31
Pen and wash over pencil
Department of Prints and Drawings
   (1927–7–21–5)
LIT: Harris 1959, plate 2; Hunt &
   Willis, plate 27 (but without Kent's
   annotations); *House in Town*, p. 27;
   Hull item 26a

Kent represents two pieces of Cardinal
Wolsey's work – the great outer
gateway or possibly 'Anne Boleyn's
Gateway' at Hampton Court and
'Wolsey's Tower' at Esher – in

conjunction with a classical building modelled upon Palladio's reconstruction of the Temple of Fortune at Palestrina, a drawing owned by Burlington (now RIBA IX/7). Harris 1959 (p.1076) and Wilson (p.154) assume that the verses inscribed around the left and bottom margins are of Kent's own composition: they are, in fact, from Michael Drayton's *Poly-Olbion*, I (1612), song 17, lines 26–72, pp.258–9: down the left margin – 'Hampton/Court/he meets the soft/ and Gentle Mole/Homes. Dale/raised hills/mole digs her/self a path/The ocean doth/return/James under/ –stood what/pains the/Mole/did take'; and at bottom left – 'the ocean doth return,/and thrusteth in the Tide/up tow'rds the place, where first his much lov'd Mole was seen./And ever since doth flow, beyond delightful Sheen'. For a full discussion of this drawing see above pp.56–7.

63 View at Claremont, with Vanbrugh's Belvedere and a classical pavilion
24 × 36
Pen and brown ink with brown wash
Department of Prints and Drawings
    (1962–7–14–51)
LIT: Hussey, plate 28; Woodbridge I, plate 24; Willis, plate 165a; Woodbridge 1981, plate 23; *House in Town*, p.93; Hull item 27

These features, viewed from the west (cf. Rocque's *Plan of Claremont*, 1738), are discussed above, p.57; the arena-like clearing before them is typically Kent.

64 Sketch of pavilion in a glade
18 × 27
Pen and grey/brown ink with wash
Department of Prints and Drawings
    (1962–7–14–47)

A very quick sketch; John Harris has suggested to me that this may be a design for Belton.

63

64

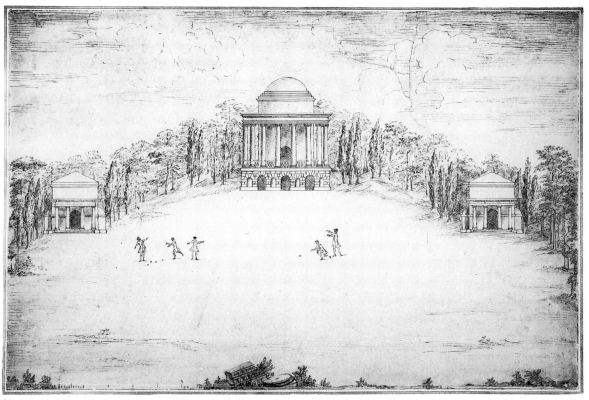

65

66 View in Pope's garden with his Shell Temple
29 × 40
Pen and ink with wash
Department of Prints and Drawings
(1872–11–9–878)
LIT: Jourdain, figure 4; Hussey, plate 20; Boutwood, figure 5; Mack 1969, plate 16; Brownell, plate 56; Hunt 1983, figure 15; Martin, plate 29; *House in Town*, p.62; Mack 1985, plate 43; Hull item 29

Probably the most published drawing by Kent, partly because it provides precious information about Pope's Twickenham garden, notably the view through the grotto to a boat on the River Thames. The Shell Temple was completed in 1725, collapsed ten years later but was apparently rebuilt, being described in 1748 as 'entirely compos'd of Shells, and consisting wholly of a Cupola or Dome, supported upon rustick Columns' (Mack 1969, pp. 239–40). Its materials associate it, despite its open temple form, with the ingredients of Italian grottoes, and it therefore provided continuity between the grotto beneath Pope's house and the garden. The flanking porches of rustic stone which Kent shows do not entirely correspond to Pope's description in the famous letter to Edward Blount (*Correspondence*, II, 296). The fanciful staffage of visiting deities, sacrificial altar and classical tripod are presumably Kent's glosses upon his friend's re-creation of an antique garden (see Hunt 1983).

65 Ionic rotunda with lawn flanked by two pavilions
34 × 51
Pen and ink with wash
Department of Prints and Drawings
(1962–7–14–49)
LIT: Woodbridge I, plate 11; Woodbridge 1981, plate 27; Hull item 34

How this has acquired (and kept: see Hull) the label of the Temple of Ancient Virtue at Stowe is a mystery; there never was as large an area as this in the Elysian Fields, nor does the lie of the land encourage its use as a bowling green as shown in this drawing. The central temple is a version of one of Kent's favourite motifs – a cross between his Stowe temple and the Mausoleum at Castle Howard. The staffage of broken classical fragments in the foreground suggests that this might be simply a *capriccio*, although it does equally have the air of an actual location.

66

67

LONDON
Lambeth Archives Department

67 Octagonal temple fronting an open space flanked by urns
15 × 21.3
Pen and wash over traces of pencil
Phillipps, III, p.78
LIT: Harris 1959, figure 7

Harris 1959 suggested this was for Esher, but has since (personal communication) more plausibly proposed that it is a design for the temple at Carlton House gardens (see above p.47).

68

68 Belvedere and grotto in landscape
30 × 43.6
Pen and ink and wash
Phillipps, III, p.76
LIT: Harris 1959, figure 6

Walpole (*Correspondence*, IX, 71) considered Esher Kent's most accomplished creation, begun soon after Henry Pelham purchased it in 1729. See cat. no. 82 for Kent's reworking of the fifteenth-century gatehouse and cat. nos 83–94 for various designs for the landscape. The gardens were laid out along the banks of the River Mole, celebrated by Kent in another drawing (cat. no. 62). Harris 1959 quotes Colley Cibber's very interesting vision of Esher as an English Tusculum with 'watered lawns and hanging groves', which this drawing partly represents. The house would be to the left of this drawing, but seems to have been excluded from the view despite the scale. The hermitage shown in Luke Sullivan's 1759 view of Esher (43, p.75) is slightly more classical than here.

69 Drawing of Claremont
41.5 × 65
Pen, ink and wash over traces of pencil
Phillipps, II, p.5

A handsome drawing, unfortunately
folded into the grangerised volume. It
is presumably a fairly finished design
for Kent's work at Claremont (Willis,
p.48, says about 1729; Hull, p.57, 'late
autumn 1734' on the basis of Robinson's
letter quoted above p.46). He
serpentined the lake, as shown here,
and created some rock work connected
to a grotto on the south-west side of
the water, which is represented here
as a more classical front. The extent of
Kent's intervention may be seen by
comparing the plan shown by Colen
Campbell in *Vitruvius Britannicus*, III,
with that by Rocque in ibid, IV. Cf.
also the painting reproduced in Harris,
The Artist and the Country House
(1979), plate 192c. The hillsides in this
drawing are considerably exaggerated;
the staffage nicely Kentian and bucolic.

LONDON
Sir John Soane's Museum

70 Stage setting with Arcadian
hermitage
30.1 × 43.5
Pen, ink and wash
In *Misc. Drawings by Robert Adam
    and others*, folio 25
LIT: Hunt 1985, plate 1

First attributed to Kent in Hunt 1985,
where it was argued that this was the
representation of some pastoral drama
or the design for one. The building
resembles both the Stowe and
Richmond hermitages; it is here
provided with the inscription
ARCADIA above the entrance. A
shepherdess and a satyr are shown just
below curved steps which, together
with the wing-like trees, suggest a
theatrical event.

69

70

71 A rustic seat or hermitage
46.5 × 30.4
Pen and wash over pencil
In *Misc. Drawings by Robert Adam
    and others*, folios 33 and 34

Despite the folio references, this is one
sheet with three items – an interior
design, an exterior elevation and a
ground plan. Here attributed to Kent.

71

LONDON
Victoria and Albert Museum

72 Temple for Euston Park, Suffolk
25.1 × 40.9
Pen and wash
V&A 3309
Inscribed in pencil in lower right-
hand corner 'J. Vardy 1755'
LIT: *Country Life* (24.i.57), plate 4;
Woodbridge I, plate 15; Wilson,
plate 90; Hull item 23. Also
illustrated in the brochure (*Drawings
by William Kent*) issued by the V&A
at the time of the small exhibition in
1984

Despite the early attribution to Vardy,
this is clearly a Kent sketch (the hounds
and horsemen are quintessentially his).
The building was erected in 1746 for
the Duke of Grafton as shown here
except for modifications to the stairs
leading up to the piano nobile. See
also cat. no. 49.

72

Cat. nos 73–80 are preliminary
drawings for engravings, 32 in all,
published after Kent's death in Thomas
Birch's 1751 edition of *The Faerie
Queene* (3 volumes). Not all drawings
were reversed. Those chosen and
presented here are a selection only of
the drawings that survive at the
Victoria and Albert Museum and the
Huntington Library, San Marino,
California; they have been selected for
their significance in an assessment of
Kent's career as a landscape designer.
Their often naive draughtsmanship,
about which Mason was particularly
severe (see above p.38) need not,
however, diminish their usefulness to
the student of Kent's landscape work.
They show a sense of recession
(especially nos. 74, 75, 76, 79, 80)
typical of landscape painting and the
illusionary stage backdrop; two (74
and 79) show double perspectives
backward into the countryside,
perhaps typical of a gardenist's

invitation to explore in different
directions. The theatrical quality of
these (and indeed others) is striking:
poses and gestures (see especially 75)
clearly reflect stage practice with its
rather stiff, formal language of the
'legible body' (see above p.34);
lighting is very contrived; a theatrical
deus ex machina appears in no.77.
Furthermore, two drawings (79 and 80)
show lakes set into landscapes very
much like some drawings at Chatsworth
(see cat. nos 31, 41 and 47) and
reinforce a sense of the inter-
changeability for Kent of landscape
and theatrical design. Kent also
suggests a specific atmosphere or
character for some individual scenes
either by a distant allusion to Serlio's
satyric scene in no.76 or the Salvator
Rosa cliché of a blasted tree trunk
(no.77). These drawings also suggest
Kent's habit of setting buildings as
single episodes in the landscape: the
fountain in 77, the building in 73 and

75. The cell of Archimago (no.73) is a
rendition of Kent's Hermitage at Stowe,
while on the island of the Idle Lake
(no.78) are a version of the Temple of
Venus at Stowe and (perhaps) the
Praeneste Terrace at Rousham, all
examples of Kent's humorous self-
reflexivity. The Chinese umbrella
(no.78), often thought of as a unique
attention on Kent's part to chinoiserie,
must now be related to the marvellous
Chinese temple among the batch of
Esher drawings (see cat. nos 90–92).
Finally, the fountain of no.77 clearly
recalls both Italian garden art and its
debts to Ovid's *Metamorphoses*, a
fascination which we know Kent
shared (see above p.38); but it was a
fascination which above all focused
upon the rivalry between art and
nature, in the case of this drawing an
artificial fountain having been
transformed from a living person and
set in a landscape which seems natural
but is highly contrived and which

73

74

bears the Rosa-like signature of the wasted tree. In no.75 the building is represented as classical in detail (pediments, columns), but detail which has a thoroughly rustic (natural) air.

The following fourteen items, largely landscape or landscape-related items for Esher Place – which Walpole rated highly (Walpole, p. 30) among Kent's designs – are selected from the group of Kent drawings, many relating to Esher, discovered by Mr John Harris and Mr Howard Colvin at Rockingham Castle, Northamptonshire, where they had gone by descent from Pelham's family; I am most grateful to their generosity in bringing these to my attention and in letting me include them in this catalogue; they have recently been acquired by the Victoria and Albert Museum, and their discovery described by John Harris 1987.

73 Illustration of *The Faerie Queene*, Book I, canto i, stanza 29
16.3 × 23.5
Pen and wash
V&A E. 871–1928
LIT: Hull item 56
Reversed when engraved (vol. I following p. 12). Annotated by Kent with reference above, names of characters to left ('Archimago/red crosse Knight/Una') and underneath the image his name, the title ('Redcross Knight & Una invited by Subtle Archimago to his Cell') and the number '2'

74 Illustration of *The Faerie Queene*, I, ii, 30
16.3 × 23.5
Pen and wash
V&A E.873–1928
Reversed when engraved (vol.I following p. 30). Annotated '1st Book' to left of drawing, together

with, first, 'Fradubio/now as tree/&
Fra Cissa a tree', and at the bottom
'ye Knight and/Fidessa/ye Knight
broke/a bough which/drops of
blood/trickled down/a yelling
voice/was heard –'

75 Illustration of *The Faerie Queene*, I,
iii, 21 ['16' in Kent's annotation]
16.3 × 23.5
Pen and wash
V&A E.874–1928
Reversed when engraved (vol.I
   following p.44). Annotated with
   incorrect reference at top, the word
   'Una' in left margin and underneath,
   between Kent's name and the
   number '5' the title, 'Una leaves the
   Old Womans House with her trusty
   Lyon after he destroyed Kirkrapine'

76 Illustration of *The Faerie Queene*, I,
vi, 14 ['7' in Kent's annotation]
16.3 × 23.5
Pen and wash
V&A E.879–1928
Reversed when engraved (vol.I,
   following p.90). Annotated at top
   with full reference, and down the
   left margin after repeating '1st Book'
   the characters 'Sylvanus/satyres
   conduct/Fair Una' and below,
   between Kent's name and '10' is
   'Una conducted by Satyrs to
   Silvanus'

75

76

1st Book

Dan Faunus

Nymph of
Diana
changd into
a Fountaine

Guyon gave
the child
to bear—
to ye Palmer

77

77 Illustration of *The Faerie Queene*, II, ii, 11
15 × 23.5
Pen and wash
V&A E.884–1928
LIT: Hull item 58
Reversed when engraved (vol.I, following p. 240). Down left margin '1st Book', 'Dan Faunus', 'Nymph of/Diana/changd into/a Fountain' and 'Guyon gave/the child/to bear —/to ye Palmer'

Phædria Guyon Black Palma   Idle Lake

78

78 Illustration of *The Faerie Queene*, II, vi, 20
16.3 × 23.7
Pen and wash; reddened on verso for transfer
V&A E.885–1928
LIT: Willis, plate 171b; Wilson, figure 58; Hull item 59; also illustrated in V&A brochure 1984
Reversed when engraved (vol.I, following p. 304). Numbered '771' at top left and '19' in lower right, and 'Phaedria Guyon Black Palma' and 'Idle Lake' below; also traces of words (cut off?) at left of drawing

79 Illustration of *The Faerie Queene*, III, vi, 28

16 × 23.5

Pen and wash; reddened on verso for transfer

Reversed when engraved (vol. II, following p. 106). Annotated '3 Book 6 Canto' at top left and 'Spencer [sic] 3d Book' in left margin with, beneath, 'Venus & Diana/seek for Cupid. found/Faire Chrysogone/and her two babes/which they took from/her Diana calld here/Belphebe. & Venus/calld here Amortta [sic]/given to Psyche to/take care of'; below drawing between Kent's name and '22' the title, 'Diana & Venus taking away Chrysogone's two Daughters Belphebe & Amoretta'

80 Illustration of *The Faerie Queene*, VI, iv, 27

16 × 23

Pen and wash

Reversed when engraved (vol. III, following p. 256). Down left margin 'Sixth/Book/4th Canto/Calepine/took the little/Babe from/the Bear/and gave it to/Matilde'; below, between Kent's name and '29' is the title 'Calepine took the Infant from ye Bear & gave it to Matilda'

81

82

81 Design for Esher in the classical taste
30 × 39
Pen and wash

Compared with the gothick building eventually designed and built (see next item), this shows that Kent could think in either style and presumably could identify different 'messages' with each style. The classical, strongly palladian, imagery here *contrasts* with the old gothic of Bishop Waynflete's gatehouse situated on lower ground toward the River Mole (at left), whereas the final, executed design specifically adds to and builds upon the original building and so maintains its visual emphasis. The gatehouse tower declares a long connection of the site with English history: the land was held by the Bishopric of Winchester from the thirteenth century; Waynflete built a new house during the third quarter of the fifteenth century; Cardinal Wolsey was imprisoned there after his fall. (See above pp.75 ff). Henry Pelham purchased Esher Place in 1729; he was brother to the Duke of Newcastle, who owned Claremont, and uncle of the owner of Oatlands, Lord Lincoln, who married Pelham's daughter. Kent, of course, worked at all three sites.

82 Gothick design for Esher and edge of park
20 × 31.5
Pen and wash over pencil

Here Kent demonstrates another solution, along the lines of that eventually adopted, whereby he adds wings to Waynflete's Tower in the gothick taste; yet even then he maintains some implicit allusions to neo-palladianism by the wing-like layout and the square end-pavilion(s) which have a less insistently mediaeval air. Kent also landscaped the territory from about 1733. In the 1701 Kip and Knyff engraving this is shown with square, compartmentalised gardens, regularly planted orchards and avenues; Kent retained an old triangular pond (personal communication from Michael Symes). Kent's alterations can be seen in Rocque's 1737 view (see 43, p.75). It was this radical change in the appearance of the ground that led Pope to write of '*Esher*'s peaceful Grove/Where *Kent* and Nature vye for PELHAM's Love'.

83

83 View in Esher Park, with temple and bridge
40 × 31 (being a sheet folded in half)
Pen and wash over (or with) pencil

A scene with many typical Kent touches: the screen of trees which invite the eye to items beyond (the cows are not inked in or have been pencilled in); the temple on the hill to left, this maintaining the classical idiom, as does the bridge over the Mole in far right which is a free version of Palladio's proposal for the Rialto Bridge. The bridge is also similar to that suggested in the Chatsworth *capriccio* (cat. no. 46).

84 View of temple
on left side of folded sheet 38 × 32
Pen over pencil

Another view, through the favourite screen of trees, of the temple seen to the left in the previous item.

84

85 Woman and sheep
on folded sheet 32 × 40
Pen and wash over pencil

Apart perhaps from the hilly terrain, there is nothing specifically to connect this with Esher. The drawing usefully suggests how Kent would have handled the edges of a wooded copse.

85

86

86 Clumps of trees and bridge over river
19 × 31.5
Pen over pencil

Again, the only reason for connecting this with Esher is its preservation with these other Esher Place drawings; perhaps it is a version of the bridge hinted at top left of the plan (cat. no. 94) or a more modest version of the bridge over the Mole (cat. no. 83).

87 A broken clump of trees with woods beyond
23.5 × 37
Pen, wash over pencil

87

This has great charm and interest,
showing Kent's concern with the
relationship of natural features
controlled by art: the art of planting,
of contrast (the two spiky firs), and
the glade opened towards the right.

88 Two designs for buildings and water
18 × 14.5
Pen over pencil

Two very quick sketches: the topmost,
of a classical temple/grotto/boathouse
at the head of a small bay, with bridge
over a stream to right; the lower, a
tent-like structure (cf. next item)
among trees at the head of a cascade
and stream. The upper sketch has some
slight parallel with cat. no. 64.

88

89

89 Design for a (? royal) tent
32 × 20
Pen and wash over pencil

Perhaps a design for some *ad hoc* festive
structure; given the crowns, lion and
unicorn, and the hint of quartered
arms, this must have been a royal
commission. It is interesting, then, for
its suggestion of Kent's contribution
to the theatrical traditions of
Renaissance princes for whom both
cityscapes and gardens were
temporarily enhanced for the
enactment of political shows.

90 Elevation and plan of Chinese
temple
27.5 × 16
Pen and wash

91 Elevation and plan of Chinese
temple
28.5 × 18
Pen and wash

92 Elevation and plan of Chinese
temple
29 × 19
Pen and wash

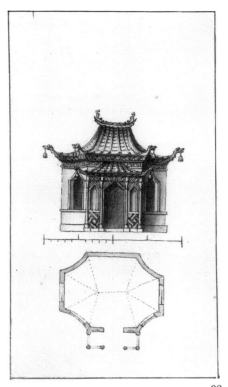

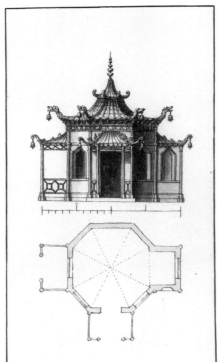

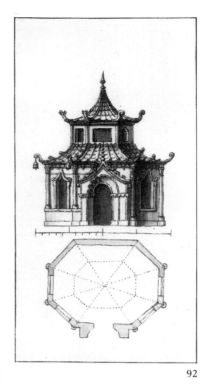

90

91

92

These three marvellous inventions are the first evidence to come to light that Kent actually designed in the Chinese taste, beginning to be popular in the 1730s (see Patrick Connor, 'China and the Landscape garden...', *Art History* II (1979), pp.429–40). All have a scale drawn underneath the elevation. If these are for Esher, they were not, as far as we know, executed.

93 Elevations and plans of belvedere
34 × 45.5
Ink and wash over pencil

Scale drawn in middle of sheet. This belvedere is almost the same as catalogue 111 (it does not have the lantern of the Wimbledon version); something like it was erected and can be seen on the hilltop of Luke Sullivan's engraved view of Esher of 1759 (54, p.90).

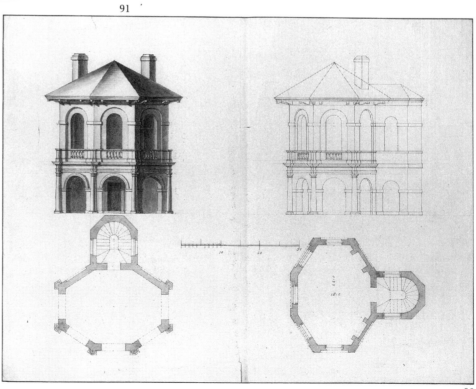

93

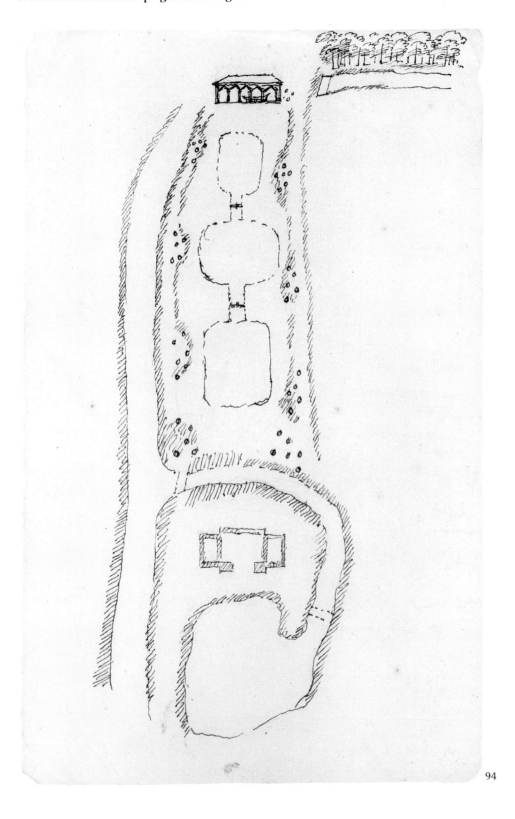

94

94 Garden plan with boathouse
32 × 26
Ink over pencil

A truly unique item – an actual plan
of a garden; though characteristically
Kent reverts to profile to depict a
boathouse (with a gondola inside) and
a screen of trees at the top right. The
sketch is unique, too, in suggesting
something of Kent's more particularised
planting ideas and supporting the claim
made by Southcote that he 'prevailed
upon Kent to resume flowers in the
natural way' (Spence, *Observations*,
p.424). The clusters of dots are
presumably studs (tubs of flowers let
into the earth, but removable at the
end of a season).

NEW HAVEN, CONNECTICUT
Yale Center for British Art

95 Deer park and house
27 × 39
Pen and wash
B.1975.2.38 (previously in collection
   of Sir Bruce Ingram Bt)
LIT: Sabin Galleries (November 1971),
   item 58; Harris 1986, figure 4

Inscribed by Kent 'a house to fodder
Deer built of wood'. The house is set
at the head of an amphitheatrical glade
and has a vaguely temple-like air; the
leaping deer are thoroughly Kentian.

a house to fodder Deer Built of wood

95

96 Design for a deer park
16.6 × 29.3
Pen and wash
B.1975.2.617 (previously in collection
    of Sir Bruce Ingram Bt)
LIT: Sabin Galleries (November 1971),
    item 59; Woodbridge I, plate 26;
    Country Houses in Great Britain,
    catalogue of exhibition at Yale
    Center, 1979, item 53; Harris 1986,
    figure 16, where dated 'about 1730'

From same source as previous item,
though the topography and the deer
house are different. Cows and sheep
(Harris 1986 says 'swine' and may be
right) have been substituted for the
deer. The change of architectural style
and the setting of the house diminish
considerably the georgic temple effect
of the other drawing.

96

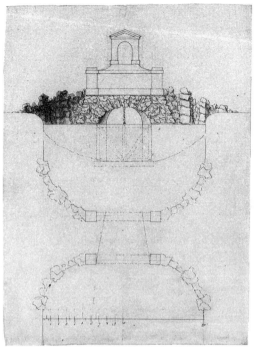

97

97 Design (plan and elevation) for the cascade at Chiswick
36.4 × 26.7
Pen and wash over pencil
B.1975.2.153
LIT: Harris 1986, figure 10

This proposal mixes a classical superstructure with a strongly rustic or natural base; cf. the various designs at Chatsworth for this crucial feature.

98

98 Design (plan and elevation) for screen and gateway
27 × 37.5
Pen and wash over pencil
B.1975.2.151
LIT: *Country Houses in Great Britain*, catalogue of exhibition at Yale Center, 1979, item 52; Rorschach, item 19; Harris 1986, figure 15

Harris 1986 suggests that this might be a 'preliminary project for the park gates at Stowe' (see Vardy, plate 50). The rather odd vista through the central arch (partly because it is not continued to left or right) has a curiously theatrical air.

99 Design (plan and elevation) for Townesend's Building, Rousham
34.5 × 24.4
Pen and wash over pencil
B.1975.2.154
LIT: Woodbridge, II, plate 7; Rorschach, item 23; Harris 1986, figure 2

The connection with Rousham is based presumably upon this design's resemblance to the temple as eventually built – without the lateral porches shown here and with other minor alterations; otherwise it seems a doubtful connection.

100 Designs (elevations and plan) for octagonal temple at Shotover Park, Oxfordshire
28.4 × 31
Pen and wash over pencil
B.1975.2.152
LIT: *Country Houses in Great Britain*, catalogue of exhibition at Yale Center, 1979, item 54; Wolterstorff, item 19, where dated 'ca.1738–45'; Harris 1986, figure 12

Besides the scale, plan and two elevations, exterior and interior, Kent also draws a piece of ornamental scrollwork with grotesque head; inscribed by Kent (on verso) with 'Coll Tyrrell/in Oxfordshire' and signed 'W.K.'. Kent designed this building and an obelisk for Colonel James Tyrrell; both still exist; both were engraved in Ware, plates 38 and 39.

101 Design for a gothick temple
35.6 × 21.6
Pen and wash over pencil
B.1981.25.360
LIT: Harris 1986, figure 17

Tentatively attributed to Kent by Harris, who compares it with the Temple of Comus in Vauxhall Gardens.

99

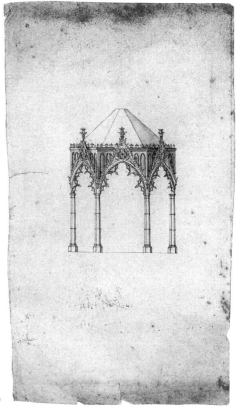

101

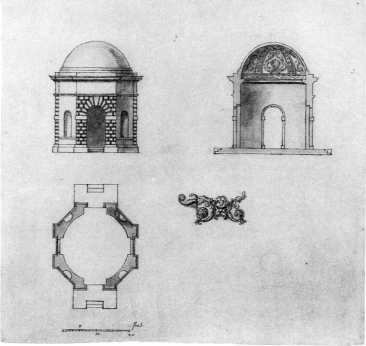

100

102

ROUSHAM, OXFORDSHIRE

104 Drawing of house as altered by Kent
20 × 33
Pen and wash
LIT: *House in Town*, p.26

A very crude and unsophisticated drawing, and its habitual attribution to Kent is somewhat optimistic (it seems more likely to be somebody's amateur rendition of a Kent sketch). It shows the battlements, ogee cupola, low side wings (but not the ogee niches actually created in the linking corridors) by which Kent remodelled the existing house into a Tudor-gothick building between 1738 and 1740. Interestingly, it also appears to show the copy of Scheemaker's statue of the Lion attacking a Horse in front of the door rather than on the top of the slope to the river (i.e. behind the artist).

OXFORD
Ashmolean Museum

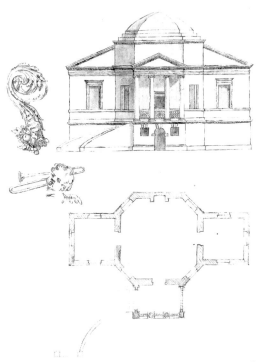

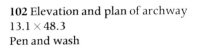

103

102 Elevation and plan of archway
13.1 × 48.3
Pen and wash

A version of the triumphal archway for Holkham; this version adds the four slit windows either side of the main archway and omits the donkey.

103 Elevation and plan of banqueting hall
39.2 × 29
Pen and wash

The design is decorated with imagery of a cherub blowing a trumpet and a scrolled leaf metamorphosing into a downward cornucopia. It has been proposed that this is for Euston (the dome but not the wings and stairs are similar to cat. no. 49).

105 Vale of Venus
27.9 × 45.7
Pen and wash over pencil
LIT: Jourdain, plate 109; Hussey, plate 205; Willis, plate 62b; Watkin, p.24; Jacques 1983, plate 9; Woodbridge II, plate 16; Woodbridge 1981, plate 20; *Zwei Jahrhunderte Englischer Malerei*, catalogue for Munich exhibition, 1980, pp.134–5; James G. Turner, 'The Sexual Politics of Landscape: images of Venus in 18th-century English poetry and landscape gardening', *Studies in Eighteenth-century Culture*, II (1982), plate 7; *House in Town*, p.65; Hunt 1986, plate 111

One of the best known of Kent's drawings, which is discussed above (pp.85 ff). As Moggridge (p.187) points out, the diminutive figures increase the size of the cascades and water spouts much more than the former are in reality (the latter are, alas, not now surviving). The openings towards the far distance to left and to right of the Venus statue are a typically Kent device, now lost through growth of trees.

104

105

106

106 View from gardens with Temple of the Mill and Eye-Catcher
34.2 × 44.4
Pen and wash over pencil
LIT: Jourdain, plate 118; Hussey, plate 215; *Zwei Jahrhunderte Englischer Malerei*, catalogue for Munich exhibition, 1980, pp. 134–136

Kent's version of his two features which draw the eye outside the gardens (though, as Moggridge has shown figure 13), there were many other opportunities for the sight to travel without artificial stimulants). For a full discussion see above, pp. 86–7. A separate design exists for the conversion of the cottage into 'The Temple of the Mill' – see cat. no. 12.

107

107 Elevation and plan of Townesend's Building
22.8 × 29.1
Pen and wash
LIT: Jourdain, plate 115; Hussey, plate 212

Presumably a first version; as built this temple, named after the builder who probably modified Kent's design, William Townesend, has a lower pitched roof and no side porches.

SHERBORNE CASTLE, DORSET

108 Gothick seat in screen of fir trees
26.4 × 48
Pen and wash
LIT: Martin, plate 48

Martin (pp.112–13) thinks that this
may be the 'Rustick Seat' seen by
Pope in 1724, but if so it would be a
very early piece of garden design. Nor
could this particular structure have
been built where Martin suggests,
since the actual ground slopes steeply
rather than being flat as Kent shows it
here. That Kent may indeed have been
invited to augment and improve
Sherborne is likely, given Pope's
enthusiasm for its various terrain and
historical associations (*Correspondence*,
II, 237ff.).

STOWE SCHOOL, BUCKINGHAMSHIRE

109 Elevation and plan of Temple of
British Worthies
31.1 × 37.46
Ink and wash
LIT: Hussey, figure 136 (elevation only);
    Hull item 35

Part of the elaborate iconography of
the Elysian Fields at Stowe, this temple
was a reworking of the original design
for the Chiswick exedra (cat. no. 34)
designed to re-house some busts from
Gibbs's Building plus some additional
ones – poets, philosophers, artists,
kings, politicians and soldiers. For a
discussion of their meaning see Clarke
1973. The drawing is annotated by
Kent with the words, 'You may hollow
this backward and make a / seat in it if
thought fit', perhaps in recollection of
the Villa Brenzone (see above p.54); in
the event the rear was used for an
inscription to a hound, 'Signior Fido'.
Scale at bottom.

108

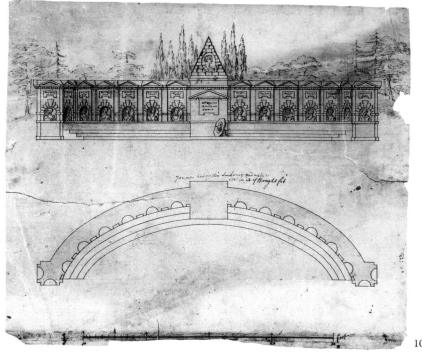

109

110

WIMBLEDON
Merton Library Service

110 Design for fishing temple
30 × 22
Pen and wash
LIT: Harris 1959, figure 8; *House in Town*, p.91

The sheet also contains a sketch for a decorative swag with goat skull and eagle (not illustrated). The two-faced god Janus shown on the top of the belvedere has led Dr Terry Friedman to suggest to me that this might be a design for the Temple of Friendship at Stowe which Walpole said was a temple of Janus. Harris 1959 says it is a fishing temple for Esher, but since this is nowhere shown on any of the newly discovered Esher drawings (see cat. nos 81–94) maybe it was not originally intended for Pelham's grounds there.

111 Elevation and plan of octagonal belvedere
21.5 × 31.5
Pen and wash over pencil
LIT: Harris 1959, figure 9 (elevation only); *House in Town*, p.91. In grangerised *History of Surrey* by W. E. Brayley

Clearly related to cat. no. 93, a hilltop temple for Esher, shown (though not as here) in Luke Sullivan's engraved view of Esher, 1759 (no.54, p.90).

111

112 Park gates with niches
23.3 × 40
Pen and wash

Some dimensions are noted on the
right-hand pier, the niche of which
does not contain a bust. The
photograph supplied by Merton
Libraries is slightly cropped and
excludes some later annotation at
bottom right.

112

113 Design for remodelling Esher Place
30 × 47
Pen and ink over pencil
LIT: Harris 1959, plate 4; Harris 1983,
     plate 2. In grangerised *History of
     Surrey* by W. E. Brayley

Two further drawings in this same
collection (ogee porch with niches,
and small building with finial balls
and niches) are not included, since the
first and probably the second are not
related to landscape projects.

113

114

PRIVATE COLLECTIONS

114 Grotto pavilion and pond for Horseheath Hall
33.3 × 24.2
Ink and wash over pencil
LIT: Sabin Galleries (November 1971) item 57; Victoria County *History of Cambridgeshire and the Isle of Ely*, VI (1978), plate facing p.64; Hull item 50

On verso – 'Ld Montford at Horseheath 1746 WK'. Henry Bromley, later Lord Mountford, employed Kent for some interior decoration at Horseheath, Linton, Cambridgeshire (see Hull p.77), so presumably Kent also designed items for the grounds at the same time. The drawing has a scale drawn along the bottom. The classical, octagonal pavilion is contrasted with a rustic, natural base. The British Library Add. MS., 5808 mentioned by Hull as having a plan of Horseheath estate on folio 168 ('possibly... made for Kent') contains details of the owner, but no plan (nor any mention of Kent).

115 The Garden of Eden
20.2 × 34.5
Pen and wash
LIT: Christie's (14 December 1982) item 101

A felicitous Kent fantasia in which the original garden is graced with a classical archway and a full repertoire of Kentian landscape devices – opening glades, winding streams, cascades, views deep into the countryside; the animals have Kent's usual whimsey, and the conspicuous elephant suggests that this might be an illustration of Milton's *Paradise Lost* (specifically Book IV, lines 140ff) where the elephant 'wreathed/His lithe proboscis' and 'murmuring waters fall/Down the slope hills ...'

115

Index

Round temple on hillside with cascade.